SIGMUND SAYS:
And Other
Psychotherapists' Quotes

SIGMUND SAYS:
And Other Psychotherapists' Quotes

Compiled by

Bernard Nisenholz
Professor Emeritus
California State University Northridge

Art work by:
Lyle Nisenholz
<u>www.lylefile.com</u>

Cover image by: George at <u>www.caricatureking.com</u>

iUniverse, Inc.
New York Lincoln Shanghai

SIGMUND SAYS: And Other Psychotherapists' Quotes

Copyright © 2006 by Bernard Nisenholz & Lyle Nisenholz

All rights reserved. No part of this book may be used or reproduced by any means, graphic, electronic, or mechanical, including photocopying, recording, taping or by any information storage retrieval system without the written permission of the publisher except in the case of brief quotations embodied in critical articles and reviews.

iUniverse books may be ordered through booksellers or by contacting:

iUniverse
2021 Pine Lake Road, Suite 100
Lincoln, NE 68512
www.iuniverse.com
1-800-Authors (1-800-288-4677)

ISBN-13: 978-0-595-39659-7 (pbk)
ISBN-13: 978-0-595-84063-2 (ebk)
ISBN-10: 0-595-39659-3 (pbk)
ISBN-10: 0-595-84063-9 (ebk)

Printed in the United States of America

Acknowledgements

Thanks to my wife Sybil for encouraging me to publish these quotations after I had put them aside, and for helping me edit the quotes that needed to be eliminated. Sybil also proofread the material. Without her help and advice, I never would have published this. Thanks to Lyle Nisenholz for contributing his artwork to this compilation.

Thanks also to Marv and Sharon Chernoff for their suggestions, and to Conrad Nisenholz, my grandson, for being Conrad Nisenholz.

Introduction

The purpose of this book is to bring together a collage of ideas, beliefs, and thoughts by many of the leading psychologists, psychiatrists, mental health counselors, marriage and family therapists, and theorists. These quotations have been chosen because they are insightful, witty, personally revealing, cleverly worded, and/or provocative. They demonstrate that the leading figures in the field are not only wise, and insightful, but also flawed and human like all of us. I have attempted to capture their wisdom and folly, both through their words and through the words of their colleagues, writers, critics, friends, and other personalities. I looked for quotations that provided some insight into the personalities and beliefs of these figures.

Wherever possible I sought out quotations that were brief. I wanted material that could say a lot in a few words, (i.e., Jung's statement "There is no birth of consciousness without pain"). I also looked for quotations representing all the major schools of psychotherapy (psychoanalytic, humanistic, and behavioral), and from individual and family therapists. From the psychoanalytic school, there are quotations by Freud, Bettelheim, Fromm, Menninger, and Reik. From the humanistic school people such as Maslow, May, Rogers, and Perls are represented. The behaviorists and cognitive behaviorists include Beck, Ellis, Lazarus, and Skinner.

Quotations have been culled from both original and secondary sources. Many have been derived from oral sources such as lectures, and utterances of colleagues and other professionals. For greater illumination I have grouped quotations together that are in striking contrast to each other or whose subject matter is directly related to each other. I have aimed at arranging quotations to present a logical flow of ideas. Many noted therapists have been left out. This was not intentional.

In order to keep the integrity and readability of the quotations I have left language usage intact. Where there is sexist language, I opted to leave such language untouched. Most of the theorists used sexist language when it was not an issue. That it is an issue now, reflects on how much cultural change has taken place.

The first topic is Freud, because it all started with Freud. Freud has influenced almost every other theory. Many theories are derivatives of Freudian thought, and many are direct reactions to it. The rest of the topics proceed alphabetically.

Readers will note that the sections on Freud and Jung are much larger than the others. This is due not only to their status, but also to the sheer volume of their writings, and others' writings about them. Both Freud and Jung wrote on many topics. Their theories are very comprehensive. In addition, Freud and Jung became rivals, and there exists much material on their relationship. I have therefore added a special section on the relationship between Freud and Jung.

Not all of the quotations are from practitioners. Two of the major figures, B. F. Skinner and Abraham Maslow are not known as psychotherapists. Each, however, has been a major influence to the field—Skinner in behavior therapy, and Maslow in humanistic psychology. Erik Erikson, although he practiced child psychoanalysis, is known mainly for his work in child development. Finally, there are figures that are mainly known for their criticism of the psychotherapeutic profession. From this group I have included quotations from Thomas Szasz, R. D. Laing, and James Hillman. Each of them has a different controversial focus. Szasz comes from a political conspiracy frame of reference, and goes so far as denying the existence of psychosis. Szasz also believes that there is no such thing as psychotherapy as a medical and scientific treatment. Laing blamed mental suffering on the debasements inherent in civilized society as interpreted by the family, and felt that allowing psychotics to pass through the psychotic process repairs the damage. There are also some quotations from famous figures outside the field of psychotherapy.

The book is educational, and useful, and can also serve as a coffee table book. The quotations can be used for speeches, lectures, writings, or simply for one's own enjoyment.

FREUD, SIGMUND (1856–1939)

The boy will come to nothing.
   Jacob Freud 1864 (After 8 year old Sigmund had relieved himself in his parents bedroom)

Almost every form of psychotherapy today is a reaction to or based on some element of Freudian thought. Freud was born in Freiberg, a small Moravian town, and died in London. Eighty years of his life, however, was spent in Vienna, Austria where he probably would have remained had not the Nazis taken over Austria in 1937. His mother had a strong and cold personality, and his father was a shadowy figure. He had four younger sisters to whom he felt superior.

The science of Psychology that was founded in 1860 by Gustav Fechner, and the work of Darwin were part of the major European movements of the time that influenced Freud. Freud came to psychology via neurology. He was trained as a physician and received his medical degree from the University of Vienna in 1881.

He began specializing in the treatment of nervous disorders. His early work was with hypnosis, which he soon rejected because he felt that its effects were only temporary, and it did not get at the root of the problem. From a Viennese physician, Joseph Breuer, he became aware of the "talking cure" which he developed. Freud developed most of the first therapeutic techniques for "talking-out" problems. He began to realize a non-physical structure of mental functioning. His investigations gradually led to the belief that there were dynamic forces at work that were responsible for creating the abnormal symptoms that he was treating, and that most of these forces were unconscious.

Freud's findings fostered a new understanding of hitherto mysterious phenomena that led to an era of greater tolerance of mental abnormality. The influence of Freud's theoretical formulations and applications permeates many aspects of contemporary culture in addition to the fields of psychology and psychotherapy. His is the most comprehensive of all psychotherapeutic theories. It includes a model of personality development, a philosophy of human nature, and a method of psychotherapy.

FREUD ON HIMSELF

A man like me cannot live without a hobbyhorse, a consuming passion—in Schiller's words a tyrant. I have found my tyrant, and in his service I know no limits. My tyrant is Psychology.

You get nothing for nothing, and you have to pay heavily for living too long! *(On his 75th birthday)*

Some rationalistic, or perhaps analytic, turn of mind in me rebels against being moved by a thing (art, music) without knowing why I am thus affected and what it is that affects me.

When someone criticizes me, I can defend myself, but against praise I am defenseless.

The (birthday) celebration evidently has sense only when the survivor can in spite of all wounds and scars join in as a hale fellow; it loses this sense when he is an invalid with whom there is no question of conviviality. And since the latter is my

case and I bear my fate by myself, I should prefer my eightieth birthday to be treated as my private affair by my friends.
(To Ernest Jones on his 80th birthday)

OTHERS ON FREUD

He (Freud) would often say three things were impossible to fulfill completely; healing, educating, and governing. He limited his goals in analytic treatment to bringing a patient to the point where he could work for a living, and learn to love.
Theodore Reik

The greatest psychopathologist has been Freud. Freud was a hero. He descended to the 'Underworld' and met their stark terrors. He carried with him his theory as a Medusa's head which turned these terrors to stone. We who follow Freud have the benefit of the knowledge he brought back with him and conveyed to us.
R. D. Laing

Freud's terminology has been misused for a purpose which Freud himself would decry—to obscure the facts.
Eric Berne

Particularly considering the state of sexual repression in late-nineteenth century Viennese society, many of Freud's insights seem hard-won and courageous as well as valid.
Carl Sagan

I think Freud would consider most analysts today nothing but picture hangers.
Eric Berne

It is one of the characteristics of a genius to have the power of vision and the courage to recognize current prejudices as such. In this sense as in others Freud certainly deserves to be called a genius.
Karen Horney

The Freudian theory is one of the most important foundation stones for an edifice to be built by future generations, the dwelling of a freer and wiser humanity.
Thomas Mann

Although the word "genius" is used indiscriminately to describe a number of people, there is no other single word that fits Freud as well as this word does. He was a genius. One may prefer to think of him, as I do, as one of the few men in history who possessed a universal mind. Like Shakespeare and Goethe and Leonardo da Vinci, whatever Freud touched he illuminated. He was a very wise man.
Calvin S. Hall

Without question Freud was a man of a thousand mistakes, many illusions, and colossal arrogance, and many of his theories are best forgotten. But the vices of great men are usually on the same scale as their virtues. Long after *Abraham Maslow, Carl Rogers,* and *Fritz Perls* are relegated to footnotes in the history of psychology, Freud will remain a permanent resident in the Hall of Exemplars.
Sam Keen

In some ways, I compare the impact of Freudian concepts with the work of Jellinek (1960), who advanced the idea that alcoholism was a disease and not the result of perversity or weakness. That, too, changed society's way of thinking and eventually led to new methods of treatment which offered hope to those who previously had no hope.
Virginia Satir

In some sense, we are all Freudians, whether we want to be or not.
Harold Bloom

The Freudian psychology is the only systematic account of the human mind which…deserves to stand beside the chaotic mass of psychological insights which literature has accumulated through the centuries.
Lionel Trilling

I see in Freud the Edison of Psychiatry, changing the descriptive to the dynamic and causal approach, and also Prometheus and Lucifer, the bearers of light.
Fritz Perls

Freud taught us—and this has not been accepted of him here because we're Americans—that life is tragic, that there are real limitations, that everything is a trade-off, that nobody can have a free lunch, that we're not getting out of this alive.
Phyllis Chesler

I just want to make one brief statement about psychoanalysis: "Fuck Dr. Freud."
Oscar Levant

Freud's greatest discovery, the one which lies at the root of psychodynamics, is that *the* great cause of much psychological illness is the fear of knowledge of oneself…We have discovered that fear of knowledge of oneself is very often isomorphic with, and parallel with, fear of the outside world.
Abraham Maslow

If you live long enough, and I hope you will, for I love life, you will see a time when Freud is no longer held to be important.
Martin Buber (Spoken to philosopher Maurice Friedman)

Freud is the father of psychoanalysis. It has no mother.
Germaine Greer

Freud is all nonsense; the secret of neurosis is to be found in the family battle of wills to see who can refuse the longest to help with the dishes. The sink is the great symbol of family life. All life is bad but family life is worse.
Julian Mitchell

Do I owe anything to *Sigmund Freud*, psychoanalyst? Today, I would say: 20 years of blindness toward the reality of child abuse as well as toward the most important facts of my life.
Alice Miller

At his best, before he recanted his correct observation that many women have been sexually abused as children, Freud taught the important lesson that a therapist should listen with care and respect for a long time to what a patient says before presuming to make interpretations.
Paula Caplan

I think he's crude, I think he's medieval, and I don't want an elderly gentleman from Vienna with an umbrella inflicting his dreams upon me.
Vladimir Nabokov

Freud knew, but ran from, the truth that most of his female patients had been sexually abused.
Peter R. Breggin

Sigmund Freud was a half-baked Viennese quack. Our literature, culture, and the films of Woody Allen would be better today if Freud had never written a word.
Ian Shoales

Freud could not separate his creation, the theory of psychoanalysis, from himself, its creator. He used his theory as a kind of loyalty oath. Rejection of any part of the theory meant personal rejection of him.
Phyllis Grosskurth

Freud's illness was that he suffered from an immense number of phobias, and as he had this illness, of course he had to avoid coping with avoidance. His phobic attitude was tremendous. He couldn't look at a patient—couldn't face having an encounter with the patient-so he had him lie on a couch, and Freud's symptom became the trademark of psychoanalysis.
Fritz Perls

While I remain dazzled by the searchlight brilliance of his mind, I regret that he did not also turn it in other directions. He looked deep *inside* the person; he hardly looked at all at the social environment.
Augustus Napier

Freud was, by his own admission, a neurotic, a diagnosis agreed with by his friend and biographer Ernest Jones. Many of Freud's early followers were themselves seriously disturbed individuals and a surprising number of them committed suicide, despite the experience of analysis and the easy availability of more. The relationship of Freud to many of his disciples was disastrous, ending with great bitterness and rancor, hardly the kind of communion therapists preach about.
Bernie Zilbergeld

His correct, conventional way of dressing, and his simple but self-assured manner, indicated his love of order and his inner serenity. Freud's whole attitude, and the way in which he listened to me, differentiated him strikingly from his famous colleagues whom I had hitherto known and in whom I had found such a lack of deeper psychological understanding. At my first meeting with Freud I had the feeling of encountering a great personality.
The Wolf-Man (Famous patient of Freud's)

He never followed them up [his cases] to see whether in actual fact what he claimed to have been successes were successful. We now know that in fact many of them were not. For Instance, the Wolfman Freud claimed to have cured was recently interviewed in Vienna. He explained that he had been treated throughout his life for the very things Freud said he had cured. Even at the age of 90 he was still suffering from the same symptoms. The claims that Freud made are simply incorrect, and one really cannot pay that much attention to them.
Hans J. Eysenck

A new round of historical research on *Sigmund Freud* is challenging the reputation of the founder of psychoanalysis. New revelations depict a Freud who seems at times mercenary and manipulative, who sometimes claimed cures where there were none, and who on occasion distorted the facts of his cases to prove his theoretical points.
Daniel Goleman (New York Times, March 6, 1990)

While Freud consciously was only a scientist and a therapist, unconsciously he was—and wanted to be—one of the great cultural—ethical leaders of the twentieth century. He wanted to conquer the world with his rationalistic-puritan dogma, and to lead man to the only—and very limited salvation—he was capable of: the conquest of passion by intellect. This, to Freud, was the *only* valid answer to the problem of man, not any kind of religion or any political solution like Socialism.
Erich Fromm

Freud, his theories, his influence are much too important for me. My admiration, bewilderment, and vindictiveness are very strong. I am deeply moved by his suffering and courage. I am deeply awed by how much, practically all alone, he achieved with the inadequate mental tools of association-psychology and mechanistically oriented philoso-

phy. I am deeply grateful for how much I developed through standing up against him.
Fritz Perls

Freud had no constructs for any system consisting of more than one person…He had no concept of experience shared by human beings.
R. D. Laing

Freud supplied to us the sick half of psychology, and we must now fill it out with the healthy half.
Abraham Maslow

Politically, he always said, 'I'm a scientist, I have nothing to do with politics,' and since politics was hooked up with sociology, I said, 'that's an impossible standpoint.' You can't be apolitical in a situation such as the world was in.
Wilhelm Reich

I believe one might find more philosophical similarity between Freud and Calvin than between Freud and Augustine.
Carl Rogers

We need to acknowledge Freud's achievements; we do not need to revere his errors. Freud was an extraordinary human being with all the failings of a man; turning him into an idol is a disservice to what must remain a continual search for truth. He taught us much; there is still much to learn.
Jeffrey Moussaieff Masson

I don't think his therapy has been the success psychoanalysts think it has.
B. F. Skinner

I confess that he [Freud] made on me personally the impression of a man obsessed with fixed ideas.
William James

Although remaining grateful for all that Freud gave us, we need to remember the fundamental cynicism and pessimism that lay at the base of his thinking.
Tom Greening

The scientific level of Freud's concept of the unconscious is exactly on a par with the miracles of Jesus. I say this despite my reverence for Freud and my admiration of his courage in insisting upon the role sex plays in the lives of all.
John B. Watson

Freud was not content with categorizing half of the human race as psychosexual cripples, reviling them as castrates. He insisted on categorizing the entire human race as psychopathic cripples, reviling them as neurotics.
Thomas Szasz

Freud, in his dying years, filled with pain and pessimism, embraced the concept of love as man's hope. It is ironic that this man who dealt with the nature of love so pitifully little in the body of his work should have embraced it, at the end of his life, as man's salvation.
Willard Gaylin

If you want to endure life, prepare yourself for death." Freud believed that the task of a therapist was to help a patient endure life. Freud's entire therapeutic career was devoted to that end. Yet, aside from this maxim, he remained mute forever about preparing for death, about the role of the concept of death in psychotherapy.
Irvin Yalom

Through all his years of pain he took no analgesic drug, and only at the end did he consent to take aspirin. He said he preferred to think in torment to not being able to think clearly.
Lionel Trilling (author and literary critic)

To us he is no more a person
Now but a climate of opinion.
W. H. Auden (Poet, on Freud's death)

FREUD AND JUNG

Jung read Freud's <u>Interpretation of Dreams</u> in 1900 while a psychiatric resident, and began a correspondence with him. Seven years later Freud and Jung met in Vienna. Freud was impressed by Jung's enthusiasm, and imagi-

nation. *They became friends and colleagues and Freud appointed Jung the first president of the International Psychoanalytic Association.*

They agreed upon the principle of the unconscious, but soon disagreed as to what the contents of the unconscious were. In 1911 Jung published <u>Symbols of Transformation</u> which challenged some of Freud's most basic ideas, and led in 1913 to a final break in their relationship. Jung took the break very hard and for a period of two years experienced a serious mid life crisis. After recovering from the critical break with Freud, Jung founded the approach known as analytical psychology.

After the parting of the ways with Freud a period of inner uncertainty began for me. It would be no exaggeration to call it a state of disorientation. I felt totally suspended in midair.
C. G. Jung

Jung is crazy, but I have no desire for separation and should like to let him wreck himself first.
Sigmund Freud (In a letter to Karl Abraham)

His attitude [Freud's] was the bitterness of the person who is entirely misunderstood, and his manners always seemed to say: 'If they do not understand, they must be stamped into hell.'
C. G. Jung

I have greatly retreated from him, and have no more friendly thoughts for him. His bad theories do not compensate me for his disagreeable character. He is following in Adler's wake, without being as consistent as that pernicious creature.
Sigmund Freud

Freud himself was neurotic his life long. I myself analyzed him for a certain very disagreeable symptom which in consequence of the treatment was cured.
C. G. Jung

The criticism with which the two heretics were met was a mild one; I only insisted that both Adler and Jung should cease to describe their theories as 'psychoanalysis'.
Sigmund Freud

I am absolutely not an opponent of the Jews even though I am an opponent of Freud's. I criticize him because of his materialistic and intellectualistic and—last but not least—irreligious attitude and not because he is a Jew. In so far as his theory is based in certain respects on Jewish premises, it is not valid for non-Jews.
C. G. Jung

Like an Old Testament prophet, he undertook to overthrow false gods, to rip the veils away from a mass of dishonesties and hypocrisies, mercilessly exposing the rottenness of the contemporary psyche. He did not falter in the face of the unpopularity such an enterprise entailed.
C. G. Jung

I had the privilege of knowing Freud personally. Despite the blatant misjudgment I have suffered at Freud's hands, I cannot fail to recognize, even in the teeth of my resentment, his significance as a cultural critic and psychological pioneer.
C. G. Jung

The relationship between Jung and Freud was a mixed marriage that could not work, and in various oblique ways, they set out to prove this to each other.
Phyllis Grosskurth

To put it simply, Freud was more ambitious and less honest about psychotherapy than Jung.
Thomas Szasz

Freud was looking for a brilliant pupil and not for a brilliant future leader. Jung was looking for an understanding father and not for a master who was eagerly looking for a successor to preserve the inheritance. Each man mistook the other, and this led to an endless crisscrossing back and forth between them which they both ignored or hid as well as or as poorly as they could.
Francois Roustang

FREUD AND WOMEN

FREUD ON WOMEN

The great question that has never been answered and which I have not yet been able to answer, despite my thirty years of research into the feminine soul, is: what *does woman want?*

Anatomy is destiny.

You must not forget, however, that we have only described women in so far as their natures are determined by their sexual function. The influence of this factor is, of course, very far-reaching, but we must remember that an individual woman may be a human being apart from this.

Psychoanalysis is for hysterical pathological cases, not for silly rich American women who should be learning how to darn socks.

But we must take care not to underestimate the influence of social conventions, which also force women into passive situations.

It must be admitted that women have but little sense of justice, and this is no doubt connected with the preponderance of envy in their mental life...We also say of women that their social interests are weaker than those of men, and that their capacity for sublimation of their instincts is less.

OTHERS ON FREUD AND WOMEN

That the equality of women was unthinkable to Freud led him to his psychology of women. I believe that his concept that half of mankind is biologically, anatomically and psychically inferior to the other half is the only idea in his thinking which seems to be without the slightest redeeming feature, except as a portrayal of a male-chauvinistic attitude.
Erich Fromm

The three most distinguishing traits of female personality were, in Freud's view, passivity, masochism, and narcissism.
Kate Millett

Freud had not the slightest understanding of sex as legitimate lust, as personal adventure, and as the potential locus for the highest degree of intimacy and respect between a man and a woman.
Thomas Szasz

Relying on the imagery of men's lives in charting the course of human growth, Freud is unable to trace in women the development of relationships, morality, or a clear sense of self. This difficulty in fitting the logic of his theory to women's experience leads him in the end to set women apart, marking their relationships, like their sexual life, as "a 'dark continent' for psychology.
Carol Gilligan

The Freudian norm of femininity, in which woman is seen as an incomplete and mutilated man, is a simple reflection of woman's traditional dilemma: to be a woman, she must behave as a mutilated person; to be a person she must see herself, and be seen by others, as a woman who mistakes herself for a man.
Miriam Greenspan

Freud himself had a hard time distinguishing the "normal" from the "neurotic" woman: they ended up looking very much alike. He admitted that the attainment of mature, normal femininity seemed to be a difficult and treacherous journey which few women completed successfully. Most women became neurotic.
Miriam Greenspan

The professional success of women analysts—including *Anna Freud* herself—had never been taken by Freud as reason to recant his general remarks, just as he had never advanced the hope that women analysts would be a vanguard of cultural change.
Elisabeth Young-Bruehl

A

ADLER, ALFRED (1870–1937)

Alfred Adler, who introduced the term, "inferiority complex," was no stranger to inferiority feelings. One of his earliest memories was sitting on a park bench when he was two years old bandaged up, suffering from rickets, and feeling helpless. In front of him his oldest brother was effortlessly running and jumping about. As he neared four years of age, his younger brother died in the bed next to his. When he was five Adler almost died from pneumonia. Perhaps in light of these experiences Adler chose medicine as his career. He graduated from the University of Vienna Medical School in 1895, and soon developed an interest in the psychological aspects of illness.

Adler was invited to join Freud's circle, The Vienna Psychoanalytic Society, after Adler wrote a defense of Freud's The Interpretation of Dreams *which had been ridiculed in the press. Adler belonged to the group for nine years, from 1902 until 1911, becoming president of the organization and editor of its journal. Soon many disagreement developed between the two on the role of early sexual trauma in mental illness, and on dream analysis. Adler was also angered by Freud's choice of Jung as president of the International Psychoanalytic Association in 1910. A series of discussions failed to reconcile their differences and Adler became the first to break with Freud. The rift between them never healed. Shortly thereafter, he formed his own group and founded his own approach called Individual Psychology.*

The rise of Nazism led to Adler's fleeing Vienna in 1935 and settling in New York. There he developed a private practice, taught at Long Island College of Medicine, wrote, and lectured all over the world.

He is often considered a bridge between the psychoanalytic and humanistic schools of psychotherapy. Adler conceptualized, and popularized such terms as birth order, inferiority feelings, and life—style.

He loved music and opera and is reported to have had a beautiful tenor voice. He was often advised to become an opera singer. He is perhaps the only psychotherapist commemorated in music. Richard Stoker, an English composer, paid tribute to Adler in a composition entitled String Quartet No. 3 (the Adlerian), Opus 36.

In the end, Adler suffered personal tragedy from political violence. His eldest daughter, Valentine, who had moved to Russia after the Nazis came to power in Germany, was arrested in February, 1937, during the Stalinist purges, never to return. Adler tried without success to intervene on her behalf. In April, 1937, he wrote, "Vali causes me sleepless nights. I am surprised how I can endure it." A few weeks later, "I cannot sleep and cannot eat. I do not know how much longer I can endure it"...A few days later, on May 28th, while on a lecture tour in Scotland, Adler died on the street of a heart attack.
Floyd Webster Rudmin

...his *gemeinschaftsgefahl,* or social interest or community feeling, moves psychology into a worldly concern, out of the private consulting room. Adler died right out in the street. What a powerful blessing.
James Hillman (Gemeinschaftsgefuhl is called by many Adlerians, as the single most unique and most important element of Adlerian psychology. It refers to one's being and feeling part of a larger social community, interested and contributing to the common welfare. This social interest is, according to Adler, necessary for mental health.)

I don't understand your sympathy for Adler. For a Jewish boy out of a Viennese suburb, a death in Aberdeen is an unheard-of career in itself and a proof of how far he had got on. The world really rewarded him richly for his service in having contradicted psychoanalysis.
Sigmund Freud (In a letter to Arnold Zweig upon hearing of Adler's death)

If Adler ever says anything sensible or worth listening to I shall take note of it, even though I don't think much of him as a person.
C. G. Jung (In a letter to Freud)

Freud employed esoteric jargon and Adler favored common sense language. One story has it that a psychiatrist took Adler to task after a lecture, denigrating his approach with the criticism, "you're only talking common sense," to which Adler replied, "I wish more psychiatrists did."
Harold H. Mosak

Dr. Adler was the kind of person the French term 'sympathique'; to talk with him was to have that rare privilege of a human relationship without barriers.... The criticism of superficiality that is leveled against some of his ideas is to an extent justified, but it is nonetheless true that his system as a whole will go down in history as a lasting contribution to the endeavor of man to understand himself.
Rollo May

ADOLESCENTS

It is normal for an adolescent to behave for a considerable length of time in an inconsistent and unpredictable manner...to be more idealistic, artistic, generous and unselfish than he will ever be again, but also the opposite; self-centered, egoistic, calculating.
Anna Freud

ADULTERY

Adultery can be a more 'healthy' recreation than for example the game of Mah Jongg or watching television.
Albert Ellis

ADULTS

Every adult...was once a child. He was once small...His triumphs will be measured against this smallness; his defeats will substantiate it.
Erik Erikson

The child wants to do what the adult does, and the adult wants to do what the child does.
Sidney Tarachow

The adult is very seldom a mature person. An adult is in my opinion a person who plays a *role* of an adult, and the more he plays the role, the more immature he often is.
Fritz Perls

AGE

The older man is particularly sensitive about his mate. If she turns him off too often, he may begin to lose his potency and go into middle-age droop, a condition which may become progressively more severe, but is nearly always reversible if put in the hands of an enthusiastic practitioner.
Eric Berne

If you're old, don't try to change yourself, change your environment.
B. F. Skinner

Age helps one to acquire some of the perspectives necessary to create harmony among apparent contradictions.
Roberto Assagioli

It is tragic when a man outlives his body.
Sigmund Freud

No one is so old as to think he cannot live one more year.
David Viscott

To the psychiatrist an old man who cannot bid farewell to life appears as feeble and sickly as a young man who is unable to embrace it.
C. G. Jung

The wine of youth does not always clear with advancing years; sometimes it grows turbid.
C. G. Jung

From the middle of life onward, only he remains vitally alive who is ready to *die with life*.
C. G. Jung

The age of patients has this much importance in determining their fitness for psychoanalytic treatment...old people are no longer educable.
Sigmund Freud

AGGRESSION

The tendency to aggression is an innate, independent, instinctual disposition in man…it constitutes the most powerful obstacle to culture.
  Sigmund Freud

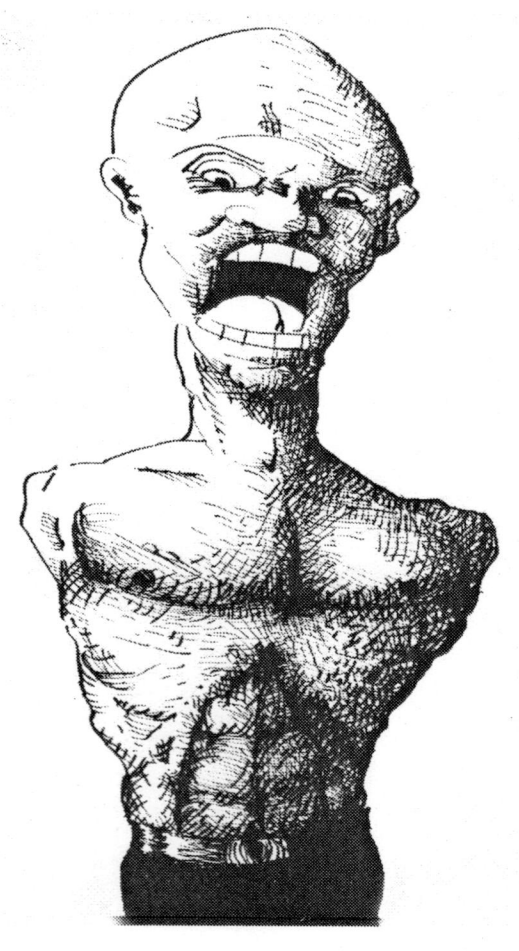

Aggression is a defensive reaction of a threatened ego.
Harry Guntrip

Impeded aggressiveness seems to involve a grave injury. It really seems as though it is necessary for us to destroy some other thing or person in order not to destroy ourselves.
Sigmund Freud

By abolishing private property one takes away the human love of aggression.
Sigmund Freud

ALIENATION/LONELINESS

Voluntary loneliness, isolation from others, is the readiest safeguard against the unhappiness that may arise out of human relations.
Sigmund Freud

The eternal problem of the human being is how to structure his waking hours.
Eric Berne

Alienation from the unconscious and from its historical conditions spells rootlessness. That is the danger that lies in wait for the conqueror of foreign lands, and for every individual who, through one-sided allegiance to any kind of—ism, loses touch with the dark, maternal, earthy ground of his being.
C. G. Jung

Oppression is the result of all human alienation.
Claude Steiner

Alienation is a retreat away from self-awareness and toward self-anesthesia.
Clark Moustakas

AMERICA/AMERICANS

America is gigantic, but it is a gigantic mistake.
   Sigmund Freud

I have always said that America is useful for nothing else but to supply money.
   Sigmund Freud

America has cost me a great deal.
   Sigmund Freud (Suffering from dyspepsia after returning from America in 1909).

Competition is much more pungent with them [Americans], not succeeding means civil death to every one, and they have no private resources apart from their profession, no hobby, games, love or other interests of a cultured person. And success means money.
   Sigmund Freud (It is ironic that although Americans were the first to bestow honors on Freud, and America ultimately was the country where psychoanalysis flourished, Freud was ferociously anti-American.)

Americans need...more therapists than the rest of the world needs because they just don't know how to be intimate...by comparison with the Europeans...they really have no deep friends to unburden themselves to.
Abraham Maslow

ANXIETY

So the formula of anxiety is very simple: anxiety is the gap between the *now* and the *then*. If you are in the now, you can't be anxious.
Fritz Perls

ART/ARTISTS

Art is almost always harmless and beneficent;...Except for a few people who are spoken of as being "possessed" by art, it makes no attempt at invading the realm of reality.
Sigmund Freud

The nature of artistic attainment is psychologically inaccessible to us.
Sigmund Freud

Art is life's dream-interpretation.
Otto Rank

An artist is once more in rudiments an introvert, not far removed from neurosis.
Sigmund Freud

No great poet or writer, no great thinker or artist has ever escaped from this deep and ultimate awareness of being somehow and somewhere rooted in nature at large.
Wilhelm Reich

AWARENESS

The aware person is alive because he knows how he feels, where he is and when it is. He knows that after he dies the trees will still be there, but he will not be there to look at them again, so he wants to see them now with as much poignancy as possible.
Eric Berne

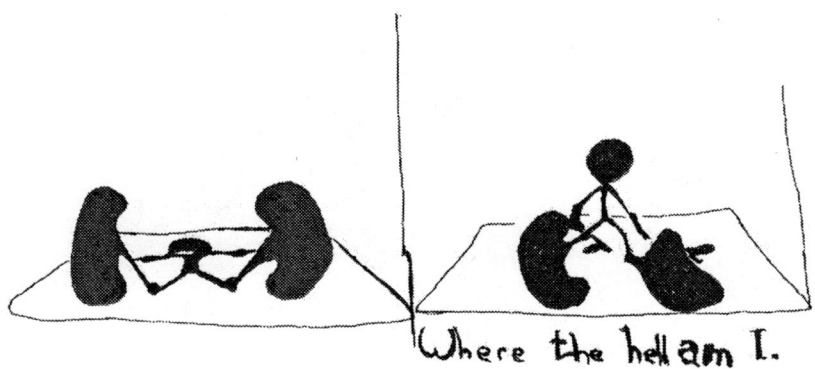

Awareness means doing away with illusions and, to the degree that this is accomplished; it is a process of liberation.
Erich Fromm

B-C

BEHAVIOR

When a man acts in such a way that he gives and receives love, and feels worthwhile to himself and others, his behavior is right or moral.
William Glasser

BEING/EXISTENCE

Man is the only animal for whom his own existence is a problem which he has to solve.
Erich Fromm

You don't have to try; you just have to be.
David Viscott

BERNE, ERIC (1910–1970)

Eric Berne contended that all children are born princes, but through parental mishandling they become frogs. Berne was certainly born a prince. He was born Eric Leonard Bernstein in Montreal, and because of anti-Semitism later changed his name to Eric Berne. Both his father and grandfather were successful physicians. Berne remained an only child until four when a sister was born. He described his father as distant, idealistic, harsh, firm, and a stern disciplinarian. He was proud of his father and often made house calls with him. At an early age Berne decided that he would also enter into medicine. When Eric was ten years old his father died from tuberculoses. His mother went to work and did all in her power to make sure that Eric remained a prince. He received a B. A. and an M. D. from Mc Gill University. He interned at Englewood Hospital in New Jersey, and then became a psychiatric resident at the Yale University Medical School. In 1941 he joined the staff of Mt. Zion Hospital in New York and began training at the New York Psychoanalytic Institute. Berne served in the Army Medical Corps from 1943 to 1946, and soon after settled in Carmel, California. He attended the San Francisco Psychoanalytic Institute and entered a training analysis with Erik Erikson. In 1956 his application for membership in the Institute was denied, possibly because of he held some unorthodox ideas.

Berne decided to pursue his own direction, and wrote a series of papers that developed the basic principles of his approach which he labeled Transactional Analysis or TA. He established a series of weekly seminars with other therapists out of which the TA movement grew. Berne was a hard worker and a prolific writer, publishing 64 articles and eight books.

TA couches much of the traditional psychodynamic thinking in a simple language that can be easily understood and learned by psychotherapists and clients. Berne conceptualized three separate ego states: Parent, Adult, and Child derived from Freud's formulation of Superego, Ego, and Id. Other terminology was decision and redecision, games, scripts, rackets, strokes, discounting, and stamps. Clients in TA develop a contract for what they want to change. They investigate their early life decisions, and discover how to redecide and initiate new directions life.

You know, I've spent my whole life teaching people how to achieve intimacy, and I've never been able to get any for myself.
Eric Berne

His approach was to shock and startle people and see what they would do. That, in a sense, was a good diagnostic opening, but it was one of the reasons why he was misunderstood in his lifetime. He antagonized people.
Fanita English

He...was really just terrible with women...In order for a woman to talk she'd have to be ten times as brilliant as a man.
Claude Steiner (In regard to Berne's seminars)

All he can tell us is that "certain fortunate people" achieve awareness, intimacy, and spontaneity. The rest, who are unprepared for this, may be better off as they are. His rather despairing conclusion is: "This may mean that there is no hope for the human race, but there is hope for individual members of it."
Edwin Schur

BIOGRAPHERS

Whoever turns biographer commits himself to lies, to concealment, to hypocrisy, to embellishments, and even to dissembling his own lack of

understanding. For biographical truth, is not to be had, and, even if one had it, one could not use it.
Sigmund Freud

BODY/BODY-MIND

Lose your mind and come to your senses.
Fritz Perls

Nobody ever thinks *too* much.
Elvin Semrad

Being in touch with the body is being in touch with the need to love.
Alexander Lowen

We have been out of touch with the body's natural environment. A mind can seem to function adequately in an office or a library, but a body needs a natural environment if it is to be alive and responsive.
Alexander Lowen

Our hearts must know the world of reason, and reason must be guided by an informed heart.
Bruno Bettelheim

BRIBERY

Only the dissatisfied and frustrated are open to bribery; only the greedy and insatiable are prone to pay bribes.
Laura Perls

CARE

Care is important because it is what is missing in our day. [There] is the seeping, creeping conviction that nothing matters; the prevailing feeling that one cannot do anything. The threat is apathy, uninvolvement, the grasping for external stimulants. Care is the necessary antidote to this.
Rollo May

CENSORSHIP

What progress we are making. In the Middle Ages they would have burnt me; nowadays they are content with burning my books.
Sigmund Freud (1933—To Ernest Jones)

CHANGE

Every human being has the chance of changing at any instant. There is the freedom to change, in principle, and no one should be denied the right to make use of it.
Viktor Frankl (Founder of Logotherapy, an approach that resulted from his experience as a prisoner in a concentration camp at the hands of the Nazis)

The experiences that change you are not always conscious.
Alexander Lowen

A human being will not change his or her personality patterns when all is said and done, until forced to do so by suffering.
Rollo May

Emptiness, depression, and death...are the concomitants of the bedrock we must reach if we are to effect change.
M. Scott Peck

CHAOS

In all chaos there is a cosmos, in all disorder a secret order.
C. G. Jung

CHARACTER

The more character a person has, the less potential he has.
Fritz Perls

CHILDREN

We can understand a child when we understand that we, too, are children at heart, on the outside a little older, perhaps a little wiser, but on the inside no different in any significant way.
Alexander Lowen

Conversing with children is a unique art with rules and meanings of its own.
Hiam Ginott (Child psychologist and author)

The moment the little boy is concerned with which is a jay and which is a sparrow, he can no longer see the birds or hear them sing.
Eric Berne

Children love and want to be loved and they very much prefer the joy of accomplishment to the triumph of hateful failure.
Erik Erikson

Permissiveness is the principle of treating children as if they were adults; and the tactic of making sure they never reach that stage.
Thomas Szasz

Adults, who all the year round deprive children of their birthright, atone by giving Christmas and birthday presents.
Laura Perls

We can keep from a child all knowledge of earlier myths, but we cannot take from him the need for mythology.
C. G. Jung

We have learned not to stunt a child's growing body with child labor; we must now learn not to break his growing spirit by making him the victim of our anxieties. If we will only learn to let live, the plan for growth is all there.
Erik Erikson

A child's greatest fear is of being unloved and abandoned by his parents.
Hiam Ginott

On the basis of early experience with the breast, the bottle, in the bedroom, kitchen and living room the child acquires his convictions, makes his decision and takes his position. Then from what he hears he chooses a prediction and a plan: how he will go about being a winner or a loser, on what grounds and what the payoff will be.
  Eric Berne

Long before a thermonuclear war can come about, we have had to lay waste our own sanity. We begin with the children. It is imperative to catch them in time. Without the most thorough and rapid brainwashing their dirty minds would see through our dirty tricks. Children are not yet fools, but we shall turn them into imbeciles like ourselves, with high I.Q.s if possible.
  R. D. Laing

CHOICE/DECISION

We who lived in concentration camps can remember the men who walked through the huts comforting others, giving away their last piece of bread. They may have been few in number, but they offer sufficient proof that everything can be taken from a man but one thing: the last of human freedoms—to choose one's attitude in any given set of circumstances, to choose one's own way.
Viktor Frankl

The fact that our lives are determined by the forces of life, is only one side of the truth; the other is that we determine these forces as our fate.
Ludwig Binswanger

You can as little choose the persons who will be the most important in your life as a traveler who enters a railway car can choose his fellow travelers.
Theodore Reik

In the important decisions of our personal lives we should be governed by the deep inner needs of our nature.
Sigmund Freud

We will the world, create it by our decision, our fiat, our choice; and we love it, give it affect, energy, power to love and change us as we mold and change it. This is what it means to be fully related to one's world.
Rollo May

The destiny of every human being is decided by what goes on inside his skull when he is confronted by what goes on outside his skull. Each person designs his own life. Freedom gives him the power to carry out his own designs, and power gives him the freedom to interfere with the designs of others. Even if the outcome is decided by men he has never met or germs he will never see, his last words and words on his gravestone will cry out his striving.
Eric Berne

A person does not act upon the world; the world acts upon him.
B. F. Skinner

Nearly all human activity is programmed by an ongoing script dating from early childhood, so that the feeling of autonomy is nearly always an illusion, an illusion which is the greatest affliction of the human race because it makes awareness, honesty, creativity, and intimacy possible for only a few fortunate individuals. For the rest of humanity, other people are seen mainly as objects to be manipulated.
Eric Berne

CHRISTIANITY

Now what we have to learn in Christianity is what the Christian mystics believe, which is that we should be concerned with serenity, with loving people, and with serving.
Rollo May

CHRISTMAS

From a symbol of man's love and justice, Christmas has degenerated into a racket, the very characteristic of which is that it throws the social process out of balance.
Laura Perls

CIVILIZATION

The principle task of civilization…is to defend us against nature.
Sigmund Freud

If the development of civilization has such a far-reaching similarity to the development of the individual and if it employs the same methods, may we not be justified in reaching the diagnosis that, under the influence of cultural urges, some civilizations…possibly the whole of mankind have become neurotic?
Sigmund Freud

COMMITMENT

Commitment is "playing for keeps."
James Bugental

CONFORMITY

*You must adjust...*This is the legend imprinted in every schoolbook, the invisible message on every blackboard. Our schools have become vast factories for the manufacture of robots.
Robert Lindner

CONFUSION

Into each life some confusion should come...also some enlightenment.
Milton Erickson

CONSCIENCE

Conscience originated when the elderly father surrounded his wives and tools with a pious taboo against his son's desires.
Sigmund Freud

A lively and vivid conscience is also the only thing that enables man to resist the effects of the existential vacuum, namely conformism and totalitarianism.
Viktor Frankl

The stars are indeed magnificent, but as regards conscience God has done an uneven and careless piece of work.
Sigmund Freud

CONSCIOUSNESS/UNCONSCIOUS

There is no birth of consciousness without pain.
C. G. Jung

The unconscious is what we do not communicate, to ourselves or to one another.
R. D. Laing (Humanistic Psychiatrist)

CONTROL

The control man has secured over nature has far outrun the control over himself.
Ernest Jones

A friend of mine returned from China and said: 'You'd love it there, people are so controlled.' What do you think happens here? People are just as much controlled in America as they are in China but the control isn't as conspicuous, that's all. We are absolutely one hundred per cent controlled in America.
B. F. Skinner

CREATIVITY

Psychoanalysis simply cannot explain creativity.
Bruno Bettelheim

Creative expression…will be forever hidden from human knowledge.
C. G. Jung

The very essence of the creative is its novelty, and hence we have no standard by which to judge it.
Carl Rogers

Does the poet create, originate, initiate the thing called a poem, or is his behavior merely the product of his genetic and environmental histories?
B. F. Skinner

There is rarely a creative man who does not have to pay a high price for the divine spark of his great gifts.
C. G. Jung

A creative person has little power over his own life. He is captive and driven by his daemon.
C. G. Jung

Creativity is not merely the innocent spontaneity of our youth and childhood; it must also be married to the passion of the adult human being, which is a passion to live beyond one's death.
Rollo May

Real creativeness, in my experience, is inextricably linked with the awareness of mortality.
Laura Perls

To create, after all, is to believe that what one says will count.
Margaret S. Mahler

Without this playing of fantasy no creative work has ever yet come to birth. The debt we owe to the play of imagination is incalculable.
C. G. Jung

The psychology of the creative is really feminine psychology, a fact which proves that creative work grows out of the unconscious depths, indeed out of the region of the mothers.
C. G. Jung

Creative minds always have been known to survive any kind of bad training.
Anna Freud

Creativity requires the courage to let go of certainties.
Erich Fromm

But creative writers are valuable allies and their evidence is to be prized highly, for they are apt to know a whole host of things between heaven and earth of which our philosophy has not yet let us dream.
Sigmund Freud

CRIME

The…deeply buried mystery of the apparent apathy to crime and to proposals for better controlling crime, lies in the persistent, intrusive wish for vengeance.
Karl Menninger

I maintain that crimes do not cease to be criminal because they have a "psychotic" motive.
Thomas Szasz

CRISIS

It is the depth of the crisis that empowers hope. The power of turning, that radically changes the situation, never reveals itself outside of crisis.
Martin Buber

D

DEATH

Death looks to me primarily like a vacation.
Roberto Assagioli

I learned to tune in on my being, my existence in the now. It was a valuable experience to face death, for in the experience I learned to face life.
Rollo May (May, contracted tuberculosis in his early thirties and was given an even chance of survival).

Death is not an act, nor even an event, for the one who dies. It is both for those who survive.
Eric Berne

What to do about death? Finish everything and then wait for like a rotting log? Or leave some things unfinished and die with regrets? The art of living is to walk the earth like a prince, scattering apples wherever you go. The art of dying is to finish your own apple just at the right moment to say, "I am content, the rest are for you to enjoy at my wake."
Eric Berne

A person cannot bear to face the prospect of inevitable death until he has had the experience of fully living...
Harold Searles

Even if death is unavoidable, however, as it is in the last analysis for everyone, there are many witnesses to testify that its contemplation can enormously enrich life.
Jerome Frank

He who would see life clearly in its final illumination must invoke death early.
Allen Wheelis

From the middle of life onward, only he remains vitally alive who is ready to *die with life*.
C. G. Jung

If you're reconciled with death or even if you are pretty well assured that you will have a good death, a dignified one, then every single moment of every single day is transformed because the pervasive undercurrent—the fear of death—is removed.
Abraham Maslow

To suffer one's death and to be reborn is not easy.
Fritz Perls

The danger arising from the inner working of the death instinct is the first cause of anxiety.
Melanie Klein

The ways we repress death and its symbolism are amazingly like the ways the Victorians repressed sex.
Rollo May

Death is death. It happens only once in a lifetime. There is no other thing in life like it. When you make this distinction, then everything except the act of death is life. To treat it any other way is a travesty on life.
Virginia Satir

…because the idea of death is subjectively inconceivable, every fear of death covers other unconscious ideas.
Otto Fenichel

Death reminds us that existence cannot be postponed.
Irvin Yalom

DEFEAT

You cannot train or condition a living being for defeat.
Alfred Adler

DEMONS

Demons do not exist any more than gods do, being only the products of the psychic activity of man.
Sigmund Freud

DEPENDENCE/INDEPENDENCE

The moment people become dependent, they are going to hate each other.
Alexander Lowen

DESTINY

Dark, unfeeling and unloving powers determine human destiny.
Sigmund Freud

DIFFICULTIES/HARDSHIPS

Man needs difficulties; they are necessary for health.
C. G. Jung

DISCOVERY

I'm someone who likes plowing new ground, then walking away from it. I get bored easily. For me, the big thrill comes with the discovering.
Abraham Maslow

DOUBT

Doubt is the brother of shame.
Erik Erikson

We want to have certainties and no doubts—results and no experiments—without even seeing that certainties can arise only through doubt and results only through experiment.
C. G. Jung

DREAMS

The dream is the most spontaneous expression of the existence of the human being. There's nothing else as spontaneous as the dream.
Fritz Perls

They (psychoanalysts) pick our dreams as though it were our pockets.
Karl Kraus

There are no indifferent dream instigators; hence, too, no innocent dreams.
Sigmund Freud

Freud once called the dream "the royal road to the unconscious." I believe that it is really the royal road to *integration*.
Fritz Perls

You analyze [people's] dreams. I try to give them the courage to dream again.
Jacob L. Moreno (spoken to Sigmund Freud)

In its very reality the dream is inaccessible.
Martin Buber

E-F

EDUCATION

Education is what survives when what has been learned has been forgotten.
B. F. Skinner

Education is learning to grow, learning what to grow toward, learning what is good and bad, learning what is desirable and undesirable, learning what to choose and what not to choose.
Abraham Maslow

A child born today in the United Kingdom stands a ten times greater chance of being admitted to a mental hospital than to a university...This can be taken as an indication that we are driving our children mad more effectively than we are genuinely educating them. Perhaps it our way of educating them that is driving them mad.
R. D. Laing

In psychotherapy and in education, giving a student full participation in the selection and process of his or her own learning [is] quite revolutionary.
Carl Rogers

Most of the universities I know think that education goes on from the neck up, and only from the neck up.
Carl Rogers

I know very few people in major universities who have any real or deep understanding of my work...universities are not interested in ways of being. They are more interested in ideas and ways of thinking.
Carl Rogers

ENEMIES

The process of enemy formation is perhaps the most devastating form of all human behavior.
M. Scott Peck

EQUALITY

True equality can only mean the right to be uniquely creative.
Erik Erikson

ERIKSON, ERIK (1902–1994)

Erik Erikson is mainly known for his work in developmental psychology. He expanded on Freud's psychosexual stages of development with an eight stage psychosocial model of the human life cycle. According to Erikson, each stage of development has its accompanying identity crisis, which most be resolved. He was more interested in the problem of what enriches and strengthens a child's ego, and not just what caused mental problems. His writings have a more hopeful and less tragic stance than that of Freud's.

Erikson was born in Frankfort, Germany and trained at the Vienna Psychoanalytic Society from 1927–1933 where he was psychoanalyzed by Anna Freud. He settled in Boston after completing his training, and became that city's first child psychoanalyst. He taught at Yale Medical School, was associated with the Institute of Child Welfare at the University of California, Berkley, and during the 1960's served as a professor of human relations at Harvard University until his retirement in 1970.

Among Erikson's books are two psychobiographies, <u>Young Man Luther</u> and <u>Gandhi's Truth</u> that demonstrate how emotional conflicts can be utilized toward constructive social ends.

Erikson was an astute observer of all the stages of the life cycle people go through from infancy through adulthood. And it was this brilliant psychoanalyst who taught me about the freedom that comes with age.
Robert Coles

He has no grasp of (or sympathy for) the political-power matrix of contemporary life. He seems to be looking at our society from a secluded country home.
Chandler Brossard

EUROPEANS

Because the European does not know his own unconscious, he does not understand the East and projects into it everything he fears and despises in himself.
 C. G. Jung

EXPECTATIONS

I do my own thing, and you do your thing.
I am not in this world to live up to your expectations
And you are not in this world to live up to mine.
You are you and I am I.
And if by chance we find each other, it's beautiful.
If not, it can't be helped.
 Fritz Perls (Gestalt Prayer)

I'm disappointed that it's so influential. I think it's had a negative effect as well as positive—a kind of 'Fuck you' attitude.
 William Schutz

With all due respect to Dr. Perls, "doing your own thing" is not enough; we cannot risk *not* seeking out those "significant others"—parents and children, sisters and brothers, husbands and wives—in our lives; we cannot risk leaving such meetings to chance and simply regretting their absence. Independence is *not* my thing. For me, full reality is *interdependence*. To achieve this goal requires risking, *seeking out*, and communicating with others.
 Everett Shostrom

It is hard to hear the famous Gestalt prayer with which Perls began his group sessions…without a twinge of embarrassment. It would be trite at any time, but seems particularly wedded to the 1960s.
 Jeffrey Moussaieff Masson

FAILURE

A failure is not always a mistake; it may simply be the best one can do under the circumstances.
 B. F. Skinner

All failures—neurotics, psychotics, criminals, drunkards, problem children, suicides, perverts, and prostitutes—are failures because they are lacking in social interest.
Alfred Adler

Losers spend time explaining why they lost. Losers spend their lives thinking about what they're going to do. They rarely enjoy doing what they're doing.
Eric Berne

FAITH

Just as a small fire is extinguished by the storm whereas a large fire is enhanced by it—likewise a weak faith is weakened by predicament and catastrophes whereas a strong faith is strengthened by them.
Viktor Frankl

People with true faith are distinguished by a quality we all recognize. That quality is grace.
Alexander Lowen

FAMILIES

Families are organisms in a continuous process of changing while trying to remain the same.
Salvatore Minuchin

All of the ingredients in a family that count are changeable and correctable.
Virginia Satir

I no longer believe in individuals; rather, I think of scapegoats, sent out by their families-of-origin to do battle with their new spouse over whose family they will recreate.
Carl Whitaker

Feelings of worth can flourish only in an atmosphere where individual differences are appreciated, mistakes are tolerated, communication is open, and rules are flexible—the kind atmosphere that is found in a nurturing family.
Virginia Satir

The man reared under and bound by authority has no knowledge of the natural law of self-regulation; he has no confidence in himself. He is afraid of his sexuality because he never learned to live naturally. Thus, he declines all responsibility for his acts and decisions, and he demands direction and guidance.
Wilhelm Reich

FEAR

We have to realize that we are as deeply afraid to live and love as we are to die.
R. D. Laing

FEELINGS

Feelings are by-products of behavior. The mistake people make is to take them as causes.
B. F. Skinner

Nature is not so wasteful as to create emotions as a nuisance. Without emotions we are dead, bored, uninvolved machines.
Fritz Perls

I also do not think feelings are important; Freud is probably responsible for the current extent to which they are taken seriously. Lytton Strachey made a comparable point about a period in French literature: The eighteenth century was supposed to be emotional, but "if anyone had asked Voltaire to analyze his feelings accurately he would have replied that he had other things to think about. The notion of paying careful attention to mere feelings would have seemed ridiculous."
B. F. Skinner

Feelings are for feeling.
Shoma Morita

FOOLS

There is a bit of Jerk in everyone.
Eric Berne

If one does not understand a person, one tends to regard him as a fool.
C. G. Jung

FORGIVENESS

The stupid neither forgive nor forget; the naive forgive and forget; the wise forgive but do not forget.
Thomas Szasz

Without forgiveness life is governed by…an endless cycle of resentment and retaliation.
Roberto Assagioli

The most famous of the unfinished situations is the fact that we have not forgiven our parents…This is part of therapy—to let go of parents, and especially to forgive one's parents, which is the hardest thing for most people to do.
Fritz Perls

FRANKL, VIKTOR (1905–1997)

Viktor Frankl developed his approach to psychotherapy, logotherapy, as a result of his experience as a prisoner in a concentration camp at the hands of the Nazis. His father, mother, brother and wife all died in camps or were sent to the gas ovens. Only he and his sister survived. His book, Man's Search for Meaning, *is a moving account of this experience, and how his philosophy developed.*

Logotherapy is based upon helping people find their meanings and purposes in life. It is Frankl's contention that, "life is unconditionally meaningful," and this meaningfulness is found, not through deliberately searching for self-satisfaction, but by fulfilling some transcendent meaning. Often this is accomplished through a work, a deed, experiencing something, or lovingly encountering others.

There are some authors who contend that meanings and values are "nothing but defense mechanisms, reaction formations and sublimations." I would not be willing to live merely for the sake of my "defense mechanisms," nor would I be ready to die merely for the sake of my "reaction for-

mations." Man, however, is able to live and even die for the sake of his ideals and values.
Viktor Frankl

A psychiatrist who personally has faced such extremity is a psychiatrist worth listening to.
Gordon Allport

Frankl is one of the most famous and gifted of all psychiatrists.... The incredible attempts to dehumanize man at Auschwitz and Dachau led Frankl to commence the humanization of psychiatry through logotherapy.
Gerald F. Kreyche

There is the story of the psychoanalyst who asked Frankl to define logotherapy in a sentence. Frankl countered by asking him to define psychoanalysis in a sentence, and the analyst said, 'In psychoanalysis, the patient lies on a couch and tells things that he finds unpleasant to tell'. 'In logotherapy', said Frankl, 'the patient sits on a chair, and hears things that he finds unpleasant to hear.'
Colin Wilson

FREEDOM

Man's freedom consists in becoming ready for accepting and letting be all that is.
Medard Boss

Freedom does not have to be achieved—it is spontaneously present in every life function. *It is the elimination of all obstacles to freedom that has to be achieved.*
Wilhelm Reich

FREUD, ANNA (1895–1982)

Anna was the youngest of Freud's six children. She entered the field of child analysis. Her first publication in 1927, <u>The Psychoanalytic Treatment of Children</u>, was an attack on Melanie Klein's theoretical approach.

I was always looking outside myself for strength and confidence but it comes from within. It is there all the time.
Anna Freud

My Anna is very good and competent.
Sigmund Freud

It is tragic that his (Freud's) daughter, who thinks that she must defend him against me, does not realize that I am serving him better than she.
Melanie Klein

She did not marry, but lived what both she and Freud recognized as a "masculine" life, thriving on the love of women and never questioning Freud's definitions of "masculine" and "feminine." She had early found the perfect man, [her father] and did not bother to seek another. Her mother was easily the least significant person in her life.
Carolyn G. Heilbrun

The most enjoyable thing near me is Anna's enjoyment in her work and her unchecked achievement.
Sigmund Freud

If Freud had fully recognized the measure of his power over his daughter, he might have hesitated to analyze her.
Peter Gay

G-H

GAMES

Games are a compromise between intimacy and keeping intimacy away.
Eric Berne

GESTAPO

I can most highly recommend the Gestapo to everyone.
Sigmund Freud (At the insistence by the Nazis that he sign a statement that they had not ill-treated him).

I would never have taken so much for a single visit.
Sigmund Freud (After the Nazis had ransacked his office in Vienna and emptied his safe.)

GLASSER, WILLIAM (1925)

William Glasser was born and raised in Cleveland where he stayed until he was twenty-eight. In 1953 he obtained his M.D. from Case Western Reserve University. He then moved to California where he founded the Institute for Reality Therapy, in Los Angeles.

Glasser believes people are born with the basic needs to be loved, and to gain self-worth and recognition. Reality therapy asks clients to examine and evaluate their behavior. Then the therapist and client work together to plan behavioral changes in order to maximize the fulfillment of needs.

At least Glasser adopts the conventional meaning of responsibility. People should be held responsible for the predictable consequences of their acts. But he is prepared to apply this notion so broadly and loosely that we end up being responsible for everything.
Edwin Schur

I understand Dr. Glasser's therapy was worked out originally in his function as psychiatrist in an institution for delinquent girls. This makes sense:...But to extend this type of therapy to every kind of patient is hopelessly to confuse the whole problem of neurosis and mental illness,

and to make the therapist society's agent for the destruction of the patient's autonomy, freedom, inner responsibility, and passion.
Rollo May

GOD

If you talk to God, you are praying; if God talks to you, you have schizophrenia.
Thomas Szasz

The stars are indeed magnificent, but as regards conscience God has done an uneven and careless piece of work.
Sigmund Freud

Whether invoked or not, God will be present.
C. G. Jung (Inscription above his front door)

Perhaps God is not dead; perhaps God is himself mad.
R. D. Laing

In the nineteenth century the problem was that God was dead; in the twentieth century the problem is that man is dead.
Erich Fromm

Like the Hasidim, just when life is heaviest with pain and anguish, that is the time when we will dance and sing together to waken the sleeping God of our own lost hope.
Sheldon Kopp

I could not say I believe. I know! I have had the experience of being gripped by something that is stronger than myself, something that people call God.
C. G. Jung

I believe there is no God and there are no devils. I don't believe that that can be absolutely proved, but that since the probability of any superhuman existence is about .0000001 or less, I choose to believe that He or She does *not* exist, until someone shows me empirical evidence to the contrary.
Albert Ellis

The Age of Enlightenment, which stripped nature and human institutions of gods, overlooked the God of Terror who dwells in the human soul.
C. G. Jung

It is just as unbearable to be God as it is to remain an utter slave.
Otto Rank

GOOD/EVIL/WICKEDNESS

It is a fact that evil cannot be denied: the wickedness of others becomes our own wickedness because it kindles something evil in our own hearts.
C. G. Jung

No patient in psychotherapy can recover his own beauty and innocence without first facing the ugliness and evil in himself.
Sheldon Kopp

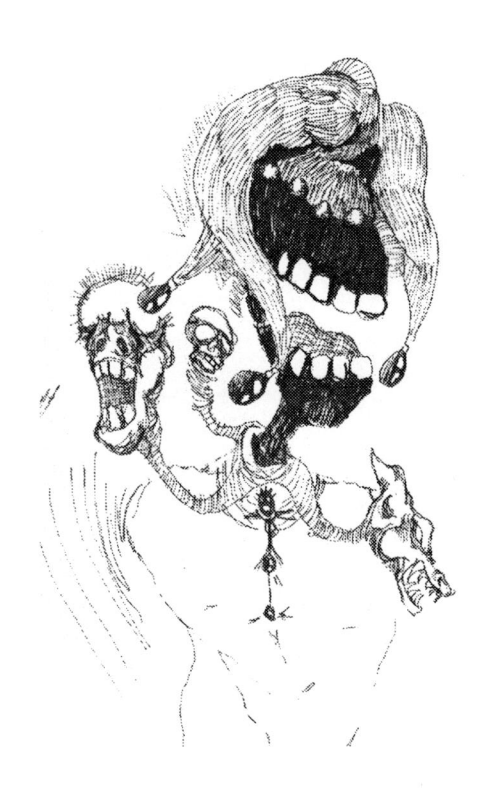

With what pleasure we read newspaper reports of crime! A true criminal becomes a popular figure because he unburdens in no small degree the consciences of his fellow men, for now they know once more where evil is to be found.
C. G. Jung

Good is all that serves life; evil is all that serves death. Good is reverence for life, all that enhances life, growth, unfolding. Evil is all that stifles life, narrows it down, and cuts it into pieces.
Erich Fromm

Modern man must rediscover a deeper source of his own spiritual life. To do this, he is obliged to struggle with evil, to confront his shadow, to integrate the devil. There is no other choice.
C. G. Jung

GREED

Greed is an expression of selfish desire which, according to Buddha's teaching, is at the root of all suffering and unhappiness. Such suffering occurs…because of the very nature of greed, which is such that no satisfaction lasts for long; it always demands something more.
Roberto Assagioli

GROWTH/SELF-ACTUALIZATION

The only reason to live is to grow, and therefore growth is worth any price.
Robert Carkhuff

We must appreciate that many people choose the worse rather than the better, that growth is often a painful process and may for this reason be shunned, that we are afraid of our own best possibilities in addition to loving them…
Abraham Maslow

We are all of us profoundly ambivalent about truth, beauty, [and] virtue, loving them and fearing them too.
Abraham Maslow

If you deliberately plan to be less than you are capable of being, then I warn you that you'll be unhappy for the rest of your life. You will be evading your own capacities, your own possibilities.
Abraham Maslow

You need not, and in fact cannot, teach an acorn to grow into an oak tree, but when given a chance, its intrinsic potentialities will develop. Similarly the human individual, given a chance, tends to develop his particular human potentialities.
Karen Horney (Psychoanalyst)

The self cannot develop unless there is freedom, choice, and responsibility.
Clark Moustakas

One cannot choose for a life unless he dares to listen to himself, *his own self*, at each moment in life…
Abraham Maslow

Many people dedicate their lives to actualize a concept of what they should be like, rather than to actualize themselves.
Fritz Perls

To live in terms of the person we are is the only way to healthy self-fulfillment. Being authentic permits us to establish a personal identity, and fosters genuine human relations.
Clark Moustakas

Every individual, every plant, every animal has only one inborn goal-to actualize itself as it is. A rose is a rose is a rose. A rose is not intent to actualize itself as a kangaroo. An elephant is not intent to actualize itself as a bird. In nature—except for the human being…growth is all one unified thing.
Fritz Perls

It is only because of problems that we grow mentally and spiritually.
M. Scott Peck

We can learn to be whole by saying what we mean and doing what we say.
Martin Buber

GUILT

Embrace your guilt rather than run from it.
Abraham Maslow

A resentment unexpressed often is experienced as, or changes into, feelings of guilt. Whenever you feel guilty, find out what you are resenting and express it and make your demands explicit. This alone will help a lot.
Fritz Perls

When we protect ourselves…from a too intensive or too quick living out or living up, we feel ourselves guilty on account of the unused life, the unlived life in us.
Otto Rank

Happiness ensues; it cannot be pursued.
Viktor Frankl

Happiness is an imaginary condition formerly often attributed by the living to the dead, now usually attributed by adults to children, and by children to adults.
Thomas Szasz

HATE/INHUMANITY

Hate is a product of the unfulfilled life.
Erich Fromm

HEDONISM

Psychiatrists should come out squarely and courageously for hedonism as a philosophical position.
Karl Menninger

HISTORY

The history of the world, which is still taught to our children, is essentially a series of race murders.
Sigmund Freud

History'll kill you.
William Glasser

HOPE

No person can live, no ego remain intact without hope and will.
Erik Erikson

HUMANKIND/MAN/MANKIND/HUMAN BEINGS

Man is the only animal for whom his own existence is a problem which he has to solve.
Erich Fromm

The only worthwhile achievements of man are those, which are socially useful.
Alfred Adler

The danger of the past was that men became slaves. The danger of the future is that men may become robots. True enough, robots do not rebel. But given man's nature, robots cannot live and remain sane.
Erich Fromm

Human beings seem to be far more autonomous and self-governed than modern psychological theory allows for.
Abraham Maslow

I now believe there is no biological, geographical, social, economic, or psychological determiner of man's condition that he cannot transcend if he is suitably invited or challenged to do so.
Sidney Jourard

We must have better human beings or else it is quite possible that we may all be wiped out and, even if not wiped out, certainly live in tension and anxiety as a species.
Abraham Maslow

Modern man must rediscover a deeper source of his own spiritual life. To do this, he is obliged to struggle with evil, to confront his shadow, to integrate the devil. There is no other choice.
C. G. Jung

Our generation is realistic, for we have come to know man as he really is. After all, man is that being who has invented the gas chambers of Auschwitz; however, he is also that being who has entered those gas chambers upright, with the Lord's Prayer or the Shema Yisrael on his lips.
Viktor Frankl

The only thing we have to fear on the planet is man.
C. G. Jung

In the depths of my heart I can't help being convinced that my dear fellowmen, with a few exceptions, are worthless.
Sigmund Freud

What man is, he has become through that cause he has made his own.
Karl Jaspers

My own belief is that man has the capacity as well as the desire to develop his potentialities and become a decent human being, and that these deteriorate if his relationship to others and hence to himself is, and continues to be disturbed. I believe that man can change and keep changing as long as he lives.
Karen Horney

An individual is just a certain uniqueness of a human being…He may become more and more individual without making him more and more human…But a person, I would say, is an individual living really with the world…This is what I would call a person and if I may say expressly yes and no to certain phenomena, I'm *against* individuals and *for* persons.
Martin Buber (In a dialog with Carl Rogers)

I think we are in the beginning of another evolution in the history of man.
Virginia Satir

In their deepest nature, human beings are causes; not simply caused.
James Bugental

A human being will not change his or her personality patterns when all is said and done, until forced to do so by suffering.
Rollo May

It is an ironic habit of human beings to run faster when we have lost our way.
Rollo May

Of course pigeons aren't people, but it's only a matter of complexity.
B. F. Skinner

I think…most men are trash.
Sigmund Freud

Human beings are not machines that have loose wires in them or burnt-out tubes that an ideal surgeon can reach and fix, or adjust, or take out, or reconnect. We are interactive, experiential organisms. *When* I respond to what goes on in a person then something goes on *in him*.
   Eugene Gendlin

We may not be what we think we are—but what we think we are will help determine what we are to become.
Willard Gaylin

A man may not always be what he appears to be, but what he appears to be is always a significant part of what he is.
Willard Gaylin

It is a matter of some irony, if one turns from psychology to one of Dostoyevsky's novels, to find that, no matter how wretched, how puerile, or how dilapidated his characters may be, they all possess more humanity than the ideal man who lives in the pages of psychiatry.
Leslie H. Farber

HUMAN NATURE

Truth and goodness and beauty are inherent in human nature. They don't have to be given to us from outside.
Abraham Maslow

If people can be educated to see the lowly side of their own natures, it may be hoped that they will also learn to understand and to love their fellow men better.
C. G. Jung

The reality of human nature is that we are—and always will be—profoundly different, for the most salient feature of human nature lies in its capacity to be molded by culture and experience in extremely variable ways.
M. Scott Peck

It is precisely the godlike in ourselves that we are ambivalent about, fascinated by and fearful of, motivated to and defensive against. This is one aspect of the basic human predicament, that we are simultaneously worms and gods.
Abraham Maslow

A little less hypocrisy and a little more tolerance towards oneself can only have good results in respect for our neighbour; for we are all too

prone to transfer to our fellows the injustice and violence we inflict upon our own natures.
C. G. Jung

We are all more simply human than otherwise.
Harry Stack Sullivan

There is no human deed or thought, which is fully outside the experience of other people.
Irvin Yalom

I believe that not only every therapeutic measure, but every single thought and act is informed by our basic conviction of what makes man "human," even if we never manifestly express this conviction and take it so much for granted that we are hardly aware of it ourselves.
Laura Perls

I-J

IDEOLOGY

Our blight is ideologies—they are the long expected Antichrist!
 C. G. Jung

IMAGINATION

Without this playing of fantasy no creative work has ever yet come to birth. The debt we owe to the play of imagination is incalculable.
 C. G. Jung

INFERIORITY

Human beings who are treated as inferior develop intensified feelings of inferiority and are likely to engage in a variety of compensatory devices in the attempt to salvage some semblance of dignity and self-esteem.
 Alfred Adler

To be human means to feel inferior.
 Alfred Adler

IGNORANCE

Ignorance is ignorance; no right to believe anything can be derived from it.
 Sigmund Freud

INFLUENCE

You can exert no influence if you are not susceptible to influence.
 C. G. Jung

INSTINCTS

Certainly man has instincts, but these instincts do not have him.
 Viktor Frankl

INSULTS

Each of us carries within himself a collection of instant insults.
 Hiam Ginott

INTEGRITY

This country, on whose coinage is written the words "In God We Trust," is also the leading manufacturer and seller of weapons in the world. What are we to do with this? Should we be perfectly comfortable about it? Should we keep these matters in separate compartments? Or should we wonder if there is a conflict between them and agonize over the tension of trying to resolve that conflict? Should we consider, for instance, with integrity, changing the inscription on our coinage to read "In Weapons We Trust" or "In God We Partially Trust."
   M. Scott Peck

JEALOUSY

Jealousy characterizes the relationship in which one seeks more power than love.
   Rollo May

JUNG, CARL GUSTAV (1875–1961)

C. G. Jung was born in Kesswil, Switzerland, the son of a Lutheran minister, and received most of his education in Basel. He remained an only child for nine years until the birth of his sister. He was a solitary child, living primarily in his imagination.

His father experienced a great deal of conflict between his religious ideology, and his personal feelings and experiences, which he was never able to reconcile. Carl felt that this led to his father's early death; as a result he distrusted any established orthodoxy.

Prior to his association with Freud, Jung formulated his own hypothesis of the unconscious psyche. He developed the first word association test in which the subject responds spontaneously to words spoken to him with the first thing that comes to mind. From the way the subjects responded to the test, Jung postulated that certain words touched a "complex"—a repressed, unconscious area of affect. The polygraph or lie detector is based upon Jung's early research.

Jung read Freud's <u>Interpretation of Dreams</u> in 1900 while a psychiatric resident, and began a correspondence with him. Seven years later Freud and Jung met in Vienna. Freud was impressed by Jung's enthusiasm, and imagination. They became friends and colleagues and Freud appointed Jung the first president of the International Psychoanalytic Association.

They agreed upon the principle of the unconscious, but soon disagreed as to what the contents of the unconscious were. In 1911 Jung published <u>Symbols of Transformation</u> in which he challenged some of Freud's most basic ideas, and led in 1913 to a final break in their relationship. Jung took the break very hard and for a period of two years experienced a serious mid life crisis.

After recovering from the critical break with Freud, Jung founded the approach known as analytical psychology. Jung objected to Freud's emphasis on sexual dynamics as determinants of behavior, and advocated a complete revision of Freud's libido theory. He also rejected Freud's basically pessimistic and deterministic view of human nature. He proposed a collective unconscious as an underlying structure of common experiences to humans as a species.

This structure included mythology, religion, primitive rituals, fairy tales, universal symbols, and various esoteric traditions. One of the major goals of Jungian psychotherapy is helping people become aware of material in their personal and collective unconscious. He formulated such terms as introvert and extrovert, the persona, the shadow, archetypes, anima and animus. Jung also stressed the importance of dreams, and the use of dream symbols. He anticipated today's transpersonal psychology and the study of altered states of consciousness. The focus of his later work concentrated on human beings in relation to the cosmos, and on understanding psychic phenomena.

Generally Jung seems to have made a greater impact upon the cultural community than upon the psychological establishment. His work is more often taught in the departments of religion and literature than in psychology. The criticism of many behavioral scientists is that Jung's theories are overly mystical and unscientific. Because Jung wrote intuitively, and allusively, the way he believed the psyche functioned, his writings present a challenge to the uninitiated. Jung's analytical psychology is now being rediscovered, especially by those interested in new age thought, Eastern religions, mysticism, and the occult.

Thank God I am Jung and not a Jungian.
 C. G. Jung

His basic concepts clearly transcended the mechanistic models of classical psychology and brought his science much closer to the conceptual framework of modern physics than any other psychological school.
 Fritjof Capra

Jung touched myth, archetype and fairy tale—the poetic truths of the human present and past.
 Edward C. Whitmont

Those who are haunted by experiences that go far beyond the "average" threaten many times to become isolated. Seldom do the words "No one understands me" come to their lips—a complaint that the old man [Jung] did in fact voice often.
 Gerhard Wehr

As a writer concerned with all the questions of the human soul and the development of human society, I consider Dr. Jung's thoughts, writings, and experimental results...a bright light in my darkness and a gold mine for reflection.
 H. G. Wells

It's often difficult to talk meaningfully about Jung because his way of expressing himself, although brilliant, is sometimes not too clear. It leaves us wondering what he really meant by many of his concepts.
 Erich Fromm

I have always had respect for Jung, but his writings have not had as much of an impression on me as those of Freud.
 Hermann Hesse

Familiarity with Jung's writings is,...indispensable for understanding the development of the pseudo religion we now call "psychotherapy."
 Thomas Szasz

...a fascistic, frothy psychoanalyst.
 Ernst Bloch

When it was pointed out to me, in connection with a criticism that I published of Jung, that Jung was enormously concerned with others because in others we find our own shadows, animas, and animuses, I replied that it was precisely this that I objected to: that he was not concerned with the other in his or her otherness, or uniqueness, but primarily in terms of the becoming of one's self.
Maurice Friedman

The name Jung seldom leaves people cold; when one mentions him, one almost always runs into emotionally loaded rejection or enthusiasm, and only rarely objective judgment.
Marie-Louise von Franz

Jung gave too much to the world and to mankind for his shadow ever to jeopardize his spiritual significance and his greatness as a man.
Aniela Jaffé (Jung's personal secretary and editor of Jung's writings)

JUNG AND THE POLITICS OF ANTI-SEMITISM

Jung underwent considerable criticism for being a Nazi sympathizer and an anti-Semite. He failed to denounce Hitler until the end of World War II. He assumed the presidency of the Nazi dominated International General Medical Society for Psychotherapy in which M. H. Göring was an active member. Jung also edited an issue of the Society's journal in which he pointed out differences between Jewish and Germanic psychology. Although Jung took serious offense to being labeled anti-Semitic, he admitted to having "slipped up" and made some errors in judgment.

JUNG ON THE JEWS

The Jew, who is something of a nomad, has never yet created a cultural form of his own and as far as we can see never will, since all his instincts and talents require a more or less civilized nation to act as host for their development.

The Jewish race, as a whole—at least this is my experience—possesses an unconscious, which can be compared with the "Aryan" only with reserve.

He [the Jew] is domesticated to a higher degree than we are, but he is badly at a loss for that quality in man, which roots him to the earth and draws new strength from below.

I am absolutely not an opponent of the Jews even though I am an opponent of Freud...In so far as his theory is based in certain respects on Jewish premises, it is not valid for non-Jews.

[Freud and Adler] are thoroughly unsatisfying to the Germanic mentality: we still have a genuine barbarian in us who is not to be trifled with, and whose manifestation is no comfort for us and not a pleasant way of passing the time...The psychotherapist with a Jewish background awakens in the German psyche not those wistful and whimsical residues from the time of David but the barbarian of yesterday, a being for whom matters suddenly become serious in the most unpleasant way. (1918)

There is no sense in us as doctors facing the National Socialist regime as if we were a party. As doctors we are first and foremost men who serve our fellows, if necessary under all aggravations of a given political situation. We are neither obliged nor called upon to make protests from a sudden access of untimely political zeal and thus gravely endanger our medical activity. (1933)

I couldn't help liking Mussolini. (1939)

There is no question but that Hitler belongs in the category of the truly mystic medicine man. (1939)

He [Hitler] was an utterly incapable, unadapted, irresponsible, psychopathic personality, full of empty, infantile fantasies, but cursed with the keen intuition of a rat or a guttersnipe. (1945)

Living as we do in the middle of Europe, we Swiss feel comfortably far removed from the foul vapours that arise from the morass of German guilt. (1945)

OTHERS ON JUNG AND JEWS

Jung praised the Nazis as long as they were winning, and when they lost the war he turned away not only from the Nazis but the whole German

people. In his personal conduct he displayed a lack of conscience and veracity.
Erich Fromm

This [Fromm above] could only have been written by one ignorant of the facts.
Gerhard Wehr

He admitted that Hitler was a phenomenon to be studied, but had only complete contempt for what he represented in every respect. He concluded by asking how anyone could truly understand the breadth of his theories concerned with understanding individuals and accuse him of being prejudiced toward believers in a religion, which reflected the wisdom of the ages.
Richard I. Evans (Reporting a conversation with Jung)

Rank also slurred Jung's character, as did others, by mistakenly considering him a Nazi sympathizer and an anti-Semite.
John P. Conger

To anyone, who, like myself, was with Jung in Berlin in July, 1933, and who saw and heard him frequently during the next twenty-eight years, the libel that Jung was a Nazi is so absurd and so entirely without foundation that it goes against the grain to take it seriously enough to contradict.
Barbara Hannah

Throughout his life,...Jung had stereotyped the Jew as rootless, burned out, overly conscious, materialistic, rationalistic, intellectualistic, abstract, and parasitic, someone unable to communicate with the chthonic qualities of the true Aryan soul. By contrast, he had stereotyped the Aryan as barbarian, youthful, creative, powerful, and dangerous, with a fantastic potential for building new cultural forms.
Clarence Karier

In the historic context of National Socialism, Jung's statements must be assessed as anti-Semitic in consequence. At the very least, he was guilty along with many others, of cultivating the intellectual climate through which the "final solution" to the Jewish problem ultimately was made possible.
Clarence Karier

It may be not accurate to say that Jung was an anti-Semite in the company of anti-Semites, and pro-Semite in the presence of anti-anti-Semites—yet there was something in his make-up that tended in this direction
Paul J. Stein

My own view is that Jung's anti-Semitism and, more important, his sympathy for fascism ran deep.
Jeffrey Moussaieff Masson

Jung's reputation, particularly at the time when my influences were being formed, was considerably tarnished by the allegation, whether it be justified or not, that he was sympathetic to the Nazi movement at the beginning and by the implication of anti-Semitism. So I've always been a bit chary of Jung in that respect though, at the same time, there is an enormous amount of stuff that Jung went over which still waits to be picked up...
R. D. Laing

JUNG ON BLACKS

The causes for the [sexual] repression can be found in the specific American Complex, namely in the living together with lower races, especially with Negroes. Living together with barbaric races exerts a suggestive effect on the laboriously tamed instinct of the white race and tends to pull it down.
C. G. Jung

In south Africa the Dutch, who were at the time of their colonizing a developed and civilized people, dropped to a much lower level because of their contact with the savage races.
C. G. Jung

With Jung, the libido became a meaningless, mystical all-soul concept, the best possible soil for the later Gleichschaltung ['equalizing'] in the Third Reich.
Wilhelm Reich

K-L

KNOWLEDGE

We can never finally know. I simply believe that some part of the human self or Soul is not subject to the laws of space and time.
C. G. Jung

The most ordinary events of the ordinary human world are beyond us.
R. D. Laing

Knowledge is a matter of degree. Any increment of knowledge or of reliability is better than doing nothing.
Abraham Maslow

The current state of psychological knowledge does not permit the development of an accurate theory of human functioning.
Arnold Lazarus

Knowledge rests not upon truth alone, but upon error also.
C. G. Jung

The best knower of the human soul will be the one who has lived through human passions himself.
Alfred Adler

The heaping together of paintings by Old Masters in museums is a catastrophe; likewise, a collection of a hundred Great Brains makes one big fat head.
C. G. Jung

KOHUT, HEINZ (1913–1981)

Heinz Kohut was born in Vienna. He received his MD from the University of Vienna in 1938. He came to the United States in 1940, and accepted a teaching position at the University of Chicago, which he held for twenty-five years. He founded the school of Self-Psychology, which placed a heavy emphasis on the mother's influence in child development. He died in 1981 of congestive heart failure.

I was Mr. Psychoanalysis. In every room I entered there were smiles. Now everybody looks away. I've rocked the boat.
Heinz Kohut

A theory has minimal truth until it is subjected to some sort of rigorous test, through empirical or phenomenological research.. Neither Erickson [Milton] nor Kohut have such a commitment to science as I feel.
Carl Rogers

Heinz Kohut, one of the latest psychoanalytic gurus, in writing about his new treatment methods, which he would have us believe are very effective, says that for some fifteen years he felt "increasingly stumped" by as many as half of his cases. Yet there was no acknowledgment of this fact in his papers written during that period. It is easy to focus on present successes and forget about past failures and just as easy not to ask why the failures weren't admitted when they were relevant.
Bernie Zilbergeld

LAING, R. D. (1927–1989)

R. D. Laing was born into a poor dysfunctional family in Glasgow, Scotland. His mother was not able to care for him initially, and his nursemaids turned out to be alcoholics. He was not allowed out of the house except on a leash until he was five. Since virtually no one was allowed in the house, a three-room apartment that was shared by his aunt and grandmother, he had no friends, and led a lonely childhood.

He did well in school and graduated from Glasgow University as a doctor of medicine in 1951. He became a psychiatrist in the British Army, worked as a physician at the Glasgow Royal Mental Hospital, and taught at the Department of Psychological Medicine at the University of Glasgow. Subsequently, he joined the Tavistock Clinic, and was late appointed Director of the Langham Clinic in London.

He came to prominence with his research with schizophrenics, different kinds of families, and with experiences under drugs such as mescaline, and LSD.

LAING ON HIMSELF

For as early as I remember I never took my self to *be* what people called me. That at least has remained crystal clear to me. Whatever, whoever I may be is not to be confused with the names people give *to* me or how they *describe* me, or what they *call* me. I am not my name.

It really seems to have stuck, this image of me as crazy. I understand that some psychiatrists have even made diagnoses based on my books.... So far I haven't been able to figure it out—what they're getting, what they're needing to get, from thinking I'm crazy.

OTHERS ON LAING

The second sweetest set of three words in English is "I don't know," and it is to R D Laing's credit that he uses it often.
    Carol Travis (On R.D. Laing's Wisdom, Madness and Folly)

Laing was a pioneer in our field. He was one of the first to explore the meaning of psychotic experience. In this sense he is comparable to Pinel who "liberated" French mental patients from the dungeon. Laing, likewise, freed contemporary psychiatric patients from the shackles of organized psychiatry.
    Kirk Schneider

Ronnie has a tremendous talent for turning things upside down in order to free you from old modes of perception.
Joan Wescott

I think that his entire life may be viewed as a passionate exploration of the "many-colored dome" of human experience—through philosophy, religion, music, and poetry; through meditation and mind-altering drugs; through his writing, his intimate contacts with schizophrenics, and his struggles with the pathologies of our society.
Fritjof Capra

LAUGHTER

The road to freedom is through laughter, and until he learns that, man will be enslaved, either subservient to his masters or fighting to serve under a new master.
Eric Berne

No comedian has ever been the head of a state for very long; the people might stand it, but he couldn't.
Eric Berne

LAW

The law is not about the truth; it's about the rules.
David Viscott (Radio show—June 1, 1992)

LEARNING

I have come to feel that the only learning which significantly influences behavior is self-discovery, self-appropriated learning.
Carl Rogers

Learning is not doing; it is changing what we do.
B. F. Skinner

Every personal encounter offers something worth learning. Any experience can be enlightening. Even a stone can be a teacher.
Sheldon Kopp

LEISURE

Leisure should be relaxing. Possibly you like complicated puzzles or chess, or other demanding intellectual games. Give them up. If you want to continue to be intellectually productive, you must risk the contempt of your younger acquaintances and freely admit that you read detective stories or watch Archie Bunker on television.
B. F. Skinner

LIFE/MEANING OF LIFE

The moment a man begins to question the meaning and value of life he is sick.
Sigmund Freud

It's an awfully risky thing—to live.
Carl Rogers (Spoken to Gloria, a client in a filmed therapy session (1965).

The chief danger in life is that you may take too many precautions.
Alfred Adler

Nothing has a stronger influence psychologically on their environment, and especially on their children, than the unlived life of the parents.
C. G. Jung

Life is not what it's supposed to be. It's what it is. The way you cope with it is what makes a difference.
Virginia Satir

There is only this life. Live it, or give it up! It does no good to choose to live it reluctantly hedging by whining that it's not sufficient, that someone must make it better for you.
Sheldon Kopp

A life never goes wrong because of a false trail; it goes wrong because the main trail is false.
Irvin Yalom

Life is not the way it's supposed to be. It's the way it is. The way you cope with it is what makes the difference.
Virginia Satir

The whole life of the individual is nothing but the process of giving birth to himself; indeed we should be fully born, when we die—although it is the tragic fate of most individuals to die before they are born.
Erich Fromm

The life of the human soul is not a 'being' but a 'becoming.'
Alfred Adler

It is quite true that man lives by bread alone-where there is no bread.
Abraham Maslow

Life is not a problem to be solved but an experience to be realized.
Karen Horney

There is no meaning to life except the meaning man gives to life by the unfolding of his powers by living productively.
Erich Fromm

The meaning of life is arrived at…by dark gropings, by feeling not wholly understood, by catching at hints and fumblings for explanations.
Alfred Adler

With the truth, one cannot live. To be able to live one needs not only illusions such as art, religion, philosophy, science and love afford, but inner illusions...
Otto Rank

The question of meaning in life is, as the Buddha taught, not edifying. One must immerse oneself in the river of life and let the question drift away.
Irvin Yalom

Man's concern about a meaning of life is the truest expression of being human.
Viktor Frankl

Human life will never be understood unless its highest aspirations are taken into account.
Abraham Maslow

Fortunately, in her kindness and patience, Nature has never put the fatal question as to the meaning of their lives into the mouths of most people. And where no one asks, no one needs to answer.
C. G. Jung

How are you able to live in a world where we are all alone, where we all die? That is very interesting. Therapists and counselors don't talk much about that.
Rollo May

For the only therapy is life. The patient must learn to live, to live with his split, his conflict, his ambivalence, which no therapy can take away, for if it could, it would take with it the actual spring of life.
Otto Rank

In creative loneliness, there is a determination to be. New feelings arise, dreams and memories, desires, and imaginings. There is often a sense of the eternal rhythms of life, a special awareness and connection with nature. Leaves and grass, earth and sky become strikingly vivid, gentle callings, whisperings to sense and feel the significance of universal ties, of the mysterious connections to color, movement, texture, and pattern to know the meaning of life and recognize the pervasive fullness in being alive now.
Clark Moustakas

It is impossible to escape the impression that people commonly use false standards of measurement—that they seek power, success and wealth for themselves and admire them in others, and that they underestimate what is of true value in life.
Sigmund Freud

Living is the fundamental business of life. We all do it only partially. Being alive is a matter of degree; not an either-or proposition.
James Bugental

Life demands compromises and half-solutions.
Theodore Reik

For only to the extent that man has fulfilled the concrete meaning of his personal existence will he also have fulfilled himself…The meaning, which a being has to fulfill, is something beyond himself, it is never just himself.
Viktor Frankl

Life comes from physical survival; but the good life comes from what we care about.
Rollo May

I am deeply convinced that the basic problem not only of therapy, but of life is how to make life livable for a being whose dominant characteristic is his awareness of himself as a unique individual on the one hand and of his mortality on the other.
Laura Perls

The shoe that fits one person pinches another; there is no recipe for living that suits all cases.
C. G. Jung

Who will tell whether one happy moment of love, or the joy of breathing or walking on a bright morning and smelling the fresh air, is not worth all the suffering and effort which life implies?
Erich Fromm

Life can be pulled by goals just as surely as it can be pushed by drives.
Viktor Frankl

As a goal in life, I think that making a lot of money is a complete washout.
Rollo May

Challenging the meaning of life is the truest expression of being human.
Viktor Frankl

To live is to be born every minute. Death occurs when birth stops.
Erich Fromm

In learning how to live, intellect is treacherous, for life is a matter of rhythms while intellect reduces rhythms to law.
Allen Wheelis

The goal of all life is death.
Sigmund Freud

All real living is meeting.
Martin Buber

For a man there are three certainties in life: death, taxes, and women. It is often difficult to say which is the worst.
Albert Ellis

LISTENING

The impact of someone's failure to listen…the absence of response has painful numbing consequences.
Clark Moustakas

It is through hearing people that I have learned all that I know about individuals, about personality, about interpersonal relationships. There is another peculiar satisfaction in really hearing someone: It is like listening to the music of the spheres, because beyond the immediate message of the person, no matter what that might be, there is the universal.
Carl Rogers

When we begin to listen to ourselves, and to listen to others, then the possibility of a dynamic peace arises.
Frank Rubenfeld

LOVE

Love is a sweet trap from which no one departs without tears.
Eric Berne

There is hardly any activity, any enterprise, which is started with such tremendous hopes and expectations and yet which fails so regularly as love.
Erich Fromm

There is a Law that man should love his neighbor as himself. In a few hundred years it should be as natural to mankind as breathing or the upright gait; but if he does not learn it he must perish.
Alfred Adler

Love, it seems, lacks scientific respectability. It has a romantic, unscientific connotation that turns psychologists off. They cannot define it without resorting to poetic ambiguities, and when a psychologist cannot define something he is in much the same position as a priest grappling with heretical doctrine: he cannot relate it to his own experience, so he sniffs suspiciously at it and pretends it is not there.
Everett Shostrom

Human beings are afraid of love and all the saccharine books to the contrary, there is reason to be afraid.
Rollo May

One must not be mean with the affections; what is spent of the fund is renewed in the spending itself.
Sigmund Freud

Love is an attempt to change a piece of dream world into reality.
Theodore Reik

One is very crazy when in love.
Sigmund Freud

The art of love…is largely the art of persistence.
Albert Ellis

What matters in relation to love is the faith in one's own love; in its ability to produce love in others, and in its reliability.
Erich Fromm

Love is a cosmic force that comes to you and exists between you and another. You do not own it.
Martin Buber

Love is more than simply being open to experiencing the anguish of another person's suffering. It is the willingness to live with the helpless knowing that we can do nothing to save the other from his pain.
Sheldon Kopp

I cannot love anyone if I hate myself. That is the reason why we feel so extremely uncomfortable in the presence of people who are noted for their special virtuousness, for they radiate an atmosphere of the torture they inflict on themselves. That is not a virtue but a vice.
C. G. Jung

We can love a person only to the extent that we are not threatened by him; we can love only if his reactions to us, or to those things which affect us, are understandable to us.
Carl Rogers

Sex wants satisfaction; love wants happiness.
Theodore Reik

Where they love they do not desire and where they desire they do not love.
Sigmund Freud

The credulity of love is the most fundamental source of authority.
Sigmund Freud

Love cannot be much younger than the lust for murder.
Sigmund Freud

Love is the immortal flow of energy that *nourishes, extends and preserves*. Its eternal goal is life.
Smiley Blanton

The main fact of life for me is love or its absence. This is a generalization for which I can think of no exception. Whether life is worth living depends for me on whether there is love in life.
R. D. Laing

To love well calls for all that is demanded by the practice of any art, indeed of any human activity, namely, an adequate measure of discipline, patience, and persistence.
Roberto Assagioli

We don't usually love a *person*. That's very, very rare. We love a certain *property* in that person, which is either identical with our behavior or supplementing our behavior, usually something that is a supplement to us.
Fritz Perls

The love for my own self is inseparably connected with the love for any other self.
Erich Fromm

M-O

MASSES/GROUPS

Masses are always breeding grounds of psychic epidemics.
C. G. Jung

A group is an obedient herd, which could never live without a master. It has such a thirst for obedience that it submits instinctively to anyone who appoints himself as its master.
Sigmund Freud

Freud's view of groups is equally pessimistic and startling. It would almost seem that Hitler must have studied and adopted these views.
Carl Rogers

MASLOW, ABRAHAM (1908–1970)

Abraham Maslow grew up in Brooklyn, New York, a Jewish boy in a non-Jewish suburb. He had few friends and spent much of his time in libraries and among books. He married at the young age of twenty, and went to the University of Wisconsin where he earned his doctorate in 1934. His dissertation was on the sexual and dominance characteristics of monkeys. He returned to New York City at a time when many of the brightest European minds escaping from Hitler, settled. Maslow studied with people such as Alfred Adler, Erich Fromm, Karen Horney, and Ruth Benedict.

Along with Carl Rogers, Rollo May, and Charlotte Buhler, Maslow founded the Association for Humanistic Psychology. He deplored the pessimism displayed by so many of the psychologists, and looked to a more positive side of humanity. He believed that human nature was essentially good, and that human beings were not inherently destructive or violent. Maslow proposed a theory of motivation based on a hierarchy of needs. At the bottom were the basic needs such as hunger and thirst, next the safety and security needs, then love and belonging, above that self-esteem, and at the top of the hierarchy growth needs leading to self-actualization such as truth, goodness, beauty, and justice.

MASLOW ON HIMSELF

With my childhood, it's a wonder I'm not psychotic.

I'm someone who likes plowing new ground, then walking away from it. I get bored easily. For me, the big thrill comes with the discovering.

I wanted to prove that humans are capable of something grander than war, prejudice, and hatred. I wanted to make science consider all the people: the best specimen of mankind I could find.

OTHERS ON MASLOW

A sugar coated Nazi
Fritz Perls

Like the more incisive of the utopians, Abe had a sense of humor about his own fantasies and an underlying sadness about the human condition. He dreamed of a grand, heroic world where all men would be strong, fulfilled, and self-actualized; where peak emotional experiences breaking the calm felicity of life would give tonus to the whole of existence; where power would be as irrelevant to all men as it was to him. But those who knew the private as well as the public man soon learned that, like all men of will and of an idea, he was also a great sufferer and was possessed by doubts about himself and his system.
Rabbi Albert S. Axelrad

More than any other person, he must be regarded as the progenitor of humanistic psychology. Maslow is destined, in my view, to be rediscovered many times before the richness of his thought is fully assimilated.
Irvin Yalom

MASTURBATION

Masturbation: the primary sexual activity of mankind. In the nineteenth century it was a disease; in the twentieth, it's a cure.
Thomas Szasz

MATURING

My formulation is that *maturing is the transcendence from environmental support to self-support.*
Fritz Perls

An adult is in my opinion, a person who plays a *role* of an adult, and the more he plays the role, the more immature he often is.
Fritz Perls

MAY, ROLLO (1909–1994)

Rollo May was one of the major influences in humanistic psychology and the existential approach to therapy. He was initially trained as a minister but became dissatisfied, and turned to psychology. He was born in Ada, Ohio. His father was a YMCA field secretary, and he grew up in a very traditional religious home. He attended Michigan State where he majored in English. After receiving his B.A. degree in 1931 he taught English at a college in Greece. During that period he visited Vienna where he attended seminars with Alfred Adler. He received a divinity degree from Union Theological Seminary in New York in 1938 where he studied under the existential philosopher, Paul Tillich. Dissatisfied with the ministry he enrolled in Columbia University in clinical psychology and earned a Ph.D. in 1949.

May's writings draw on Greek mythology, world literature, philosophy, art, and religion for ideas, examples, and metaphors.

An Existentialist without an existence.
Fritz Perls

…one of the most penetrating observers of human experience.
James Bugental

MEN/MALES

The dominance of man over woman deprived him of the highest sexual pleasures and must in a more highly developed civilization lead women to rebellion against their feminine role.
Alfred Adler

Men generally are not candid in sexual matters. They do not show their sexuality freely, but they wear a thick overcoat—a fabric of lies—to conceal it, as though it were bad weather in the world of sex.
Sigmund Freud

Man's potential thoughts, feelings, wishes and fantasies know no bounds, save those set by his biological structure and his personal history. But the male role, and the male's self-structure will not allow man to acknowledge or to disclose the entire breadth and depth of his inner experience to himself or to others.
Sidney Jourard

MEANING

Meanings are discovered not invented.
Viktor Frankl

My impression is that if I try to find the meaning of my own experience it leads me to directions regarded as absurd.
Carl Rogers

There is only one meaning to each situation, and that is its true meaning.
Viktor Frankl

MENTAL HEALTH/MENTAL ILLNESS

Show me a sane man and I will cure him for you.
C. G. Jung

Mental health problems do not affect three or four out of every five persons but one out of one.
William Menninger

A person who is mentally ill is a creator who got stuck.
Zerka Moreno

Experience shows without a doubt that when once a poor man has produced a neurosis it is only with difficulty that he lets it be taken from him. It renders him too good a service in the struggle for existence; the secondary gain from illness, which it brings him, is much too important. He now claims by right of his neurosis the pity, which the world has refused, to his

material distress, and he can now absolve himself from the obligation of combating his poverty by working.
Sigmund Freud

Almost all psychic distress is the product of a distorted perception that transforms our present reality, undervalues our strengths and anticipates a dreaded imagined doom that tragically may arrive—precisely and only because it is anticipated.
Willard Gaylin

The deepest need of man…is the need to overcome his separateness, to leave the prison of his aloneness. The *absolute* failure to achieve this aim means insanity.
Erich Fromm

Everybody is a little sick; nobody is really sick, and no one knows what mental sickness really is anyhow.
Willard Gaylin

The sicknesses of the soul are sicknesses of relationship. They can only be treated completely if I transcend the realm of the patient and add to it the world as well.
Martin Buber

The neurotic cannot will without guilt.
Otto Rank

Insanity—a perfectly rational adjustment to an insane world.
R. D. Laing

I envy paranoids; they actually feel people are paying attention to them.
Susan Sontag

It sometimes takes a crazy man to see the insanity in our culture.
Alexander Lowen (Speaking of Wilhelm Reich).

Mystics and schizophrenics find themselves in the same ocean, but the mystics swim whereas the schizophrenics drown.
R. D. Laing

Thus the neurotic character represents not illness but a developmental phase of the individuality problem, a personality denying its own will, not accepting itself as an individual.
Otto Rank

A considerable number of persons are able to protect themselves against the outbreak of serious neurotic phenomena only through intense work.
Karl Abraham

The concept of mental illness is analogous to that of witchcraft. In the fifteenth century, men believed that some persons were witches, and that some acts were due to witchcraft. In the twentieth century, men believed that some people are insane, and that some acts are due to mental illness.
Thomas Szasz

At times people have said that madness is something to be admired, or that the mad and eccentric are more creative and alive than other people. They are said to be the rebels in a repressive society.... The mad are failures, and failure is not admirable. To encourage madness, as some enthusiasts do, is to encourage failure.
Jay Haley

Neurosis is always a substitute for legitimate suffering.
C. G. Jung

Neurosis seems to be a human privilege.
Sigmund Freud

The neurotic is not only emotionally sick—he is cognitively wrong.
Abraham Maslow

Doubt is to certainty as neurosis is to psychosis. The neurotic is in doubt and has fears about persons and things; the psychotic has convictions and makes claims about them. In short, the neurotic has problems, the psychotic has solutions.
Thomas Szasz

Neurotic means he is not as sensible as I am, and psychotic means he's even worse than my brother-in-law.
Karl Menninger

The crazy person says, "I am Abraham Lincoln," and the neurotic says, "I wish I were Abraham Lincoln," and the healthy person says, "I am I, and you are you."
Fritz Perls

Neurosis and psychosis are modes of expression for human beings who have lost courage.
Alfred Adler

The neurotic type has taken into himself potentially the whole of reality.
Otto Rank

Neurotic behavior is quite predictable. Healthy behavior is unpredictable.
Carl Rogers

[The neurotic] is much nearer to the actual truth psychologically than the others and it is just that from which he suffers.
Otto Rank

The neurotic can be cured if only he can be induced to abandon his retreat from people and achievements.
Rudolph Dreikurs

The neurotic must dismantle his defenses and go back to where he made the disastrous decision to act out of the expectations of others rather than out of his own feelings.
Arthur Janov

In our Western world, the neurotic is the man who cannot face his own dying and therefore cannot live fully as a human being.
Laura Perls

The moment of the outbreak of neurosis is not just a matter of chance; as a rule it is most critical. It is usually the moment when a new psychological adjustment, that is, a new adaptation, is demanded.
C. G. Jung

Theatrical performances require an audience. They are not lived for their own sake alone. So too with neurosis.
Sheldon Kopp

Acquaintance with a culture, which in many ways is different from the European taught me to realize that many neurotic conflicts, are ultimately determined by cultural conditions.
Karen Horney

We must not forget to include the influence of civilization among the determinants of neuroses. It is easy, as we can see, for a barbarian to be healthy: for a civilized man the task is a hard one.
Sigmund Freud

That millions of people share the same forms of mental pathology does not make these people sane.
Erich Fromm

Many people get diagnosed as psychotics, not on the basis of their behavior or maladjustment, but on the basis of the content of their experiences.
Stanislav Grof

Usually when we talk about the psychopath we are talking about the unsuccessful psychopath. The reason why we generally do not discuss the successful psychopath is because we would then have to discuss many of the rulers of our world.
Harold Greenwald

Among political leaders a high degree of narcissism is very frequent; it may be considered an occupational illness, or asset, especially among those who owe their power to their influence over mass audiences.
Erich Fromm

Society highly values its normal man. It educates children to lose themselves and to become absurd, and thus to be normal.
Normal men have killed perhaps 100,000,000 of their fellow normal men in the last fifty years.
R. D. Laing

In over 100 cases where we studied the actual circumstances around the social event when one person comes to be regarded as schizophrenic, it seems to us that *without* exception the experience and behavior that gets labeled schizophrenic is a *special strategy that a person invents in order to live in an unlivable situation.*
 R. D. Laing

Our common world is to the schizophrenic a world of illusions, conventions. Their particular world is the real one. They even have a double stream of memory.
 Martin Buber

Generous people are rarely mentally ill people.
 Karl Menninger

A person cannot bear to face the prospect of inevitable death until he has had the experience of fully living, and the schizophrenic has not yet fully lived.
 Harold Searles

Depression is a loss of an organism's internal force comparable in one sense to the loss of air in a balloon or tire.
 Alexander Lowen

Studies show that 80% of the population suffers from depression and 20% of you caused it.
 Dana Eagle

It would appear that once precipitated into psychosis the patient has a course to run. He is, as it were, embarked upon a voyage of discovery, which is only completed by his return to the normal world, to which he comes back with insights different from those of the inhabitants who never embarked on such a voyage.
 Gregory Bateson

It is the pampered child, Adler would say, who is willing to play only so long as the universe plays his or her way. The healthy individual, on the other hand, is willing to walk the knife-blade edge of insecurity and to

affirm truth and goodness even though truth is on the scaffold and goodness is never perfectly achieved.
Rollo May

Absence of psychoneurotic illness may be health, but it is not life.
D. W. Winnicott

A Freudian slip is when you say one thing but mean your mother.
(Anonymous)

If we admit our depression openly and freely, to those around us, we get from it an experience of freedom rather than the depression itself.
Rollo May

Many an attack of depression is nothing but the expression of regret at having to be virtuous.
Wilhelm Stekhel

Masochists are people who changed their spears into boomerangs that, returning, struck them.
Theodore Reik

MIND/INTELLECT/REASON/PSYCHE

In learning how to live, intellect is treacherous, for life is a matter of rhythms while intellect reduces rhythms to law.
Allen Wheelis

The mind is an iceberg; it floats with only one-seventh of its bulk above water.
Sigmund Freud

Mind is the essence of being alive.
Gregory Bateson

The voice of the intellect is a soft one, but it does not rest until it has gained a hearing. Ultimately, after endless rebuffs, it succeeds. This is one of the few points in which one may be optimistic about the future of mankind.
Sigmund Freud

Where *id* was, there shall ego be.
Sigmund Freud

There is no place in a scientific analysis of behavior for a mind or self.
B. F. Skinner

We must completely give up the idea of the psyche being somehow connected with the brain.
C. G. Jung

MINUCHIN, SALVADOR (1921)

Salvador Minuchin, one of the leaders in the development of family therapy, was born of a Jewish family in Argentina. As a young man he was arrested and spent three months in jail for protesting the Peron government. Eventually he immigrated to Israel. He came to the United States in 1950 and worked with delinquent boys at the Wiltwick School in New York. He founded the Structural school of family therapy, whose main center is the Philadelphia Child Guidance Clinic.

Minuchin's approach is concerned with the hierarchy of a family's organization. Pathology occurs when there is confusion in the hierarchy or when the rules are broken. The structural family therapist intervenes in the hierarchy by forming strategic coalitions with various family members. The aim is to help the family outgrow stereotypical patterns, and to restructure the family system.

A growing number of people in the field questioning the implicit sexual politics in family therapy practice have accused Minuchin of reinforcing sex stereotypes.
Richard Simon

If they [feminists] are saying I am a knee-jerk chauvinist who doesn't understand the social context in which families live, they are wrong.
Salvatore Minuchin

More than anyone Minuchin established the legitimacy of family therapy within psychiatry.
Phil Guerin

Life is supposed to be disorderly, boring, fragmented, repetitive, in need of drastic editing. Watching a Minuchin session, or a tape of it, is like being at a tightly constructed, well directed, magnificently acted play.
Janet Malcolm

The thing I most admire about Sal is the way he developed techniques for helping those [poor] families when nobody else could.
Peggy Papp

MOTHERS

The precursor of the mirror is the mother's face.
D. W. Winnicott

Very early in the life of most children food becomes identified with love. To eat becomes an expression of love; not to eat is an expression of rebellion. Very often the child realizes that not eating is one way to get back at an obsessive mother.
Alexander Lowen

MYTHOLOGY

We can keep from a child all knowledge of earlier myths, but we cannot take from him the need for mythology.
C. G. Jung

P

PARENTS/PARENTING

People should choose their parents more wisely.
Harry Stack Sullivan

The world talks to the mind. Parents speak more intimately—they talk to the heart.
Hiam Ginott

Nothing has a stronger influence psychologically on their environment, and especially on their children, than the unlived life of the parents.
C. G. Jung

Being a parent is the ultimate training in humility; you cannot be a parent without failing.
Salvatore Minuchin

The most famous of the unfinished situations is the fact that we have not forgiven our parents...This is part of therapy; to let go of parents, and especially to forgive one's parents, which is the hardest thing for most people to do.
Fritz Perls

But as no child will develop courage by being overprotected, so no child will develop it by being pushed.
Rollo May

It is wise to remember that rebellion belongs to the freedom you have given your child by bringing him or her up in such a way that he or she exists in his or her own right. In some instances it could be said: "you sowed a baby and you reaped a bomb.' In fact this is always true, but it does not always look like it.
D. W. Winnicott

Whenever a child lies you will find a severe parent. A lie would have no sense unless truth was felt to be dangerous.
  Alfred Adler

PATIENTS/CLIENTS

The patient needs an experience, not an explanation.
  Frieda Fromm-Reichman

For the mental patient's family and society, mental illness is a 'problem'; for the patient himself it is a 'solution.'
Thomas Szasz

Why should I tolerate a perfect stranger at the bedside of my mind?
Vladimir Nabokov

It is a categorical demand of the patient's life plan that he should fall through the guilt of others and thus be free from responsibility.
Alfred Adler

Patients aren't warehoused in snake pits any longer. They sit instead in wretched welfare hotels and Bowery flophouses. The shopping-bag ladies and other casualties wander the streets, prey for all the vultures, until they are harmed or in some other way attract the attention of law-enforcement authorities. Then they are sent back to the state hospitals; cleaned up; pushed through the revolving door back into the community.
William Rubin

Anything that increases the patient's feeling of responsibility for his own words must tend to cure him.
Helmuth Kaiser

Knowledgeable moderns put their back to the couch and in so doing may occasionally fail to put their shoulders to the wheel.
Allen Wheelis

We must remember that every 'mental' symptom is a veiled cry of anguish. Against what? Against oppression, or what the patient experiences as oppression. The oppressed speak a million tongues.
Thomas Szasz

No patient in psychotherapy can recover his own beauty and innocence without first facing the ugliness and evil in himself.
Sheldon Kopp

People who come to therapy suffer from lies, either lies they have been told by their parents, their siblings, their teachers, the media, or lies they have told themselves.
M. Scott Peck

Patients are nothing but riff-raff. The only useful purposes they serve are to help us earn a living and to provide learning material. In any case, we cannot help them.
Sigmund Freud (Remark made to Sandor Ferenczi)

Remember that the buyer of mental health services must be very wary and highly selective. Like choosing a lifelong companion, it can be the most important choice, for better or worse that you'll ever make.
Peter R. Breggin

It has been my experience that persons have a basically positive direction. In my deepest contacts with individuals in therapy, even those whose troubles are most disturbing, whose behavior has been most antisocial, whose feelings seem most abnormal, I find this to be true.
Carl Rogers

For the only therapy is life. The patient must learn to live, to live with his split, his conflict, his ambivalence, which no therapy can take away, for if it could, it would take with it the actual spring of life.
Otto Rank

PERCEPTION

We live in the world as we perceive it. The size of one's life is the size of one's perceived world.
James Bugental

Any experience which is inconsistent with the organization or structure of self may be perceived as a threat, and the more of these perceptions there are, the more rigidly the self-structure is organized to maintain itself.
Carl Rogers

PERLS, FRITZ (1893–1970)

Fritz Perls, the founder of Gestalt therapy, was born in Berlin, the third child of Jewish parents. His eldest sister was legally blind, and particularly unattractive; she clung a great deal to her mother. He disliked his eldest sister and resented the attention given to her by his mother and by his second sister. He also hated his father and what he called "his pompous righteousness." His father was stern, autocratic, and referred to his son as, "a piece of shit."

Perls rebelled against the rigid discipline and anti-Semitism of the school he attended, as well as the rote memory work required, by becoming unmanageable. In spite of this he was a brilliant student. He attended medical school and served as a medical corpsman in World War I. After the War he earned his doctorate in medicine from Frederick Wilhelm University in 1921.

Perls studied psychoanalysis and went to work for Kurt Goldstein, a leading proponent of Gestalt psychology, in Frankfort at the Institute for Brain Damaged Soldiers. There he met his wife Laura. Together, they conceptualized Gestalt therapy.

Perls trained with Wilhelm Reich in the early thirties, and was influenced by Reich's theory of character armor, a physical counterpart of psychological trauma. When the Nazis came to power in 1933, the Perls and their two-year-old daughter escaped to Amsterdam for a short while. They then moved to South Africa where they settled and established therapeutic practices. They came to New York in 1946 and organized the New York Institute for Gestalt Therapy. Fritz separated from Laura and moved to the West Coast in 1960. In 1964 he became a resident workshop leader and cult figure at Esalen Institute in Big Sur. In 1969 he established a Gestalt commune on Lake Cowichan, Vancouver Island, British Columbia, and founded the Gestalt Institute of Canada.

Perls was a powerful personality. He demanded honesty from everyone. He had a reputation as a ruthless healer. He often acted spontaneously with clients alternately showing loving tenderness, impatience, anger, and interest. People both feared and respected him. Jack Gaines, a Gestalt therapist, tells about Perls once falling asleep while working with a patient in a Gestalt workshop. The patient had been flatly rambling on about his problems when he suddenly realized that Perls was dozing. He complained about paying good money to come to the workshop, and expected Perls to pay attention to him. Perls slightly opened his eyes, reached into his pocket, pulled out a twenty-dollar bill, handed it to the man and fell asleep again.

Gestalt therapy is an experiential therapy that emphasizes here-and-now awareness, direct experience, and the responsibility of the client for his or her own behavior and experience. It is an abstraction based upon existentialism, Gestalt psychology, Zen Buddhism, Reichian character armor, and psychoanalysis.

The crazy *Fritz Perls* is becoming one of the heroes in the history of science.
Fritz Perls

The thing Fritz found most difficult to accept about himself was his lack of perfection. Thus, in spite of his writing, "Friend, don't be a perfectionist, be proud of your mistakes," he always strove for perfection.
William Schutz

Fritz's liabilities, real as they were, seem unimportant when placed on a ledger alongside of his assets. In a way, these very shortcomings are what gave the man character, drama, and humanness. Imperfections, boldly accepted, are the truest acceptance of the human condition.
Martin Shepard

He was, for me, a perfect animal-not in a low but in a high sense. He could be nasty or funny, crude or kind, lewd or loving, cheap or extravagant, *and he didn't bother to hide any of it.* He encompassed as broad a range of emotions and responses as anyone I have ever met, the "negative" as well as the "positive" ones.
Martin Shepard

Though Perl's words leave no doubt that he was highly sensitive to the issue of responsibility and cognizant of the fact that the therapist must not accept the burden of the patient's responsibility, he was never able to solve (or for that matter, I believe, to recognize fully) the paradox of his approach to therapy. "Assume responsibility." the patient is told. "And I'll tell you precisely how, when and why to do it.".. To receive two simulta-

neous, conflicting messages, one explicit and the other implicit, is to be placed in a classical double bind.
Irvin Yalom

Fritz was a bastard and contradictory...
Jim Simkin

I think there was a lot of unfinished business in his life. There was unfinished business with me, and a great deal of unfinished business with his father. His father humiliated him continually...And any kind of criticism, not just from me, would devastate him and reactivate the original reaction to his father. As a result, he would always escape from criticism in some way. He also escaped from comparison with others. He always started something new and was the generator.
Laura Perls

For some years I felt somewhat resentful that he (Fritz) never acknowledged my collaboration in the whole development of Gestalt therapy.
   Laura Perls (Laura who conceptualized much of Gestalt theory never received the credit or earned the fame that Fritz earned at least partly because she wrote little and did not publish, and partly because Fritz took all the credit.)

I also heard a story about the last words *Fritz Perls* uttered before he died, which may or may not be true...He was in a hospital and he sat up in the hospital bed, although he had many tubes in him. The nurse came in and said, "Dr. Perls you lie down this instant. You shouldn't be up like this." And he said, as I hear the story, "Nobody tells *Fritz Perls* what to do." And then he died.
Ram Dass

Perls was an aged womanizer with a vulgar tongue and enormous ego. With his large, unkempt beard and predilection for jumpsuits, Perls strolled around Esalen as if he owned it.
Edward Hoffman

Perls made no bones about abrogating to himself all the privileges and power of the traditional guru. Implicit in this power is the ability to cause great pain and destruction to others, either directly or by causing the group to turn on, attack, and brutalize one of its members. Perls

seemed positively to revel in the power he held over the people in his groups.
Jeffrey Moussaieff Masson

Perls was incapable of close, enduring relationships, his therapy work was often at odds with what he said it should be like, and the arrogant, browbeating way he dealt with many of his clients was poles apart from what he and other therapists recommend to people.
Bernie Zilbergeld

PERMISSIVENESS

Permissiveness is the principle of treating children as if they were adults; and the tactic of making sure they never reach that stage.
Thomas Szasz

PERSONALITY

A personality is a full Congress of orators and pressure groups, of children, demagogues, communists, isolationists, warmongers, mug-wumps, grafters, log-rollers, lobbyists, Caesars and Christs, Machiavels and Judases, Torries and Promethean revolutionists.
Henry A. Murray

PIGEONS

If I could do it all over again, I'd never teach those pigeons to play ping-pong.
B. F. Skinner (Skinner experimented with positive and negative reinforcement on laboratory animals, including pigeons, in order to predict and control their behavior. His experiments with pigeons during World War II was aimed at training them to perform such tasks as guiding missiles, bombs, and torpedoes to intercept and destroy enemy aircraft. His plan, although feasible, was never implemented.)

PLAY

Play is the exultation of the possible.
Martin Buber

POWER

The lust for power is not rooted in strength but in weakness.
    Erich Fromm

Power abdicates only under stress of counter power.
    Martin Buber

Never underestimate the power of a single individual. Remember one candle in a cave lights everything.
    Abraham Maslow

PRESENCE

When I sit with someone, I know that is something, even if I have nothing valuable to say. I no longer need constant evidence that I am being effective and helpful. I can just sit and give my company. I have been in situations where my pain could not be understood, and I have taken comfort just being with someone willing to be with me, someone who required nothing, could not grasp my torn-up feelings but was human company-like a place to go when you are down and out, a human presence, civilization after wilderness.
    Eugene Gendlin

What we are missing! What opportunities of understanding we let pass by because at a single, decisive moment we were, with all our knowledge, lacking in the simple virtue of a *full human presence!*
    Karl Jaspers

PRINCIPLES

It is easier to fight for one's principles than to live up to them.
    Alfred Adler

PROMISES

The man who promises everything is sure to fulfill nothing, and everyone who promises too much is in danger of using evil means in order to carry out his promises, and is already on the road to perdition.
    C. G. Jung

PSYCHOLOGY

The science that tells you what you already know in words you don't understand.
Anonymous

Modern psychology has lost the vision of life and growth; instead, it is preoccupied with psychopathology and conditioned responses.
Sheldon Kopp

PSYCHOLOGISTS

Psychologists are a much more fearful group than other scientists—they tend to stick with problems that can be resolved with rats.
Carl Rogers

PSYCHOTHERAPY/PSYCHIATRY/COUNSELING

Therapy should be like a poker game; the result is what counts.
Eric Berne (Founder of Transactional Analysis)

Essentially, psychotherapy is an authentic meeting between human beings.
R. D. Laing

In psychotherapy, enthusiasm is the secret of success.
C. G. Jung

Psychotherapy is a matter of communicating experience, not a matter of imparting objective information.
R. D. Laing

Fortunately, analysis is not the only way to resolving inner conflicts. Life itself remains a very effective therapy.
Karen Horney

No therapist should ever believe "My therapy is the way." Nor should we believe that therapy in general is the only way.
Peter R. Breggin

So in psychotherapy and in education, giving a student full participation in the selection and process of his or her own learning—that's quite revolutionary.
Carl Rogers

We must grudgingly admit that even as we were trying to devise, with scientific determinism, a therapy for the few, we were led to promote an ethical disease among the many.
Erik Erikson

Psychotherapy is the only form of treatment, which, at least to some extent, appears to create the illness it treats.
Jerome Frank

Psychotherapy is not a panacea. It never was, and I do not believe it ever will be. Psychotherapy comprises a specialized set of techniques, applicable to specific circumstances and conditions, and no more.
Hans Strupp

Most therapists are convinced that it is their method and insight that produces patient improvement, but this is not true. Any improvement is probably the result of the placebo effect.
Arthur K. Shapiro

It's pretty hard to know what you're doing in psychotherapy because most of it is about at the level of the University of Paris faculty of medicine in the sixteenth century when people were using a lot of big words and they were having a lot of staff conferences, but none of the patients were getting better.
Eric Berne

The task of therapy is to arouse (remind) forgotten desires; to fire up abandoned conflict; and to keep all combatants at the front until everyone wins.
Walter Kempler

The goal of my therapy is eccentricity.
James Hillman

I decided to become a psychoanalyst, I married the profession for better or for worse.
Theodore Reik

Man basically *is* free, and any man can come to learn and to grow and to become the free person he is. This is the purpose of counseling—to help the individual to loosen himself from his deterministic shackles, and to come to realize and to see what he has always had—choice and freedom.
Dugald S. Arbuckle

Psychotherapy cannot be reformed in its parts, because the activity, by its nature, is harmful. Recognizing the lies, the flaws, the harm, the potential for harm, the imbalance in power, the arrogance, the condescension, the pretensions may be the first step in the eventual abolition of psychotherapy that I believe is, one day in the future, inevitable and desirable.
Jeffrey Moussaieff Masson

My business is turning frogs into princes.
Eric Berne

Only frogs want to be princes or princesses...people want to become human beings and the job in therapy is to get patients out of fairy tales and into life.
Mary Goulding

It is not transference but direct feeling of pain that is curative.
Arthur Janov

Psychotherapy can be viewed as a social institution created to fill the gap left by the decay of other institutions that gave meaning to life and a feeling of connectedness to others.
Jerome Frank

My own philosophy is based on the conviction that people have within themselves the resources and capacity for self-understanding and self-correction. The goal of therapy as I see it, is to create the proper climate so self-discovery and personal growth can take place.
Carl Rogers

But the sacred place of the work (psychotherapy) is not paid for by the fee, nor defined by personal limitations. It is the place, rather, of the depth of the therapist's being, and the client's...In traditional language, it is the place given by the grace of God.
Stephen Schoen

...by removing the soul from the world and not recognizing that the soul is also in the world, psychotherapy can't do its job anymore.
James Hillman

All psychotherapy must end in impasse if it does not provide for political consciousness.
Anthony Wilden

What psychotherapy at its best can do is well captured by an old French maxim: "To cure sometimes, to help often, to comfort and console always." Therapy in our time can do no more—we will be lucky if it can do this much—and in the long run neither clients nor therapists benefit by pretending otherwise.
Bernie Zilbergeld

The structure of psychotherapy is such that no matter how kindly a person is, when that person becomes a therapist, he or she is engaged in acts that are bound to diminish the dignity, autonomy, and freedom of the person who comes for help.
Jeffrey Moussaieff Masson

And therapy, in its crazy way, by emphasizing the inner soul and ignoring the outer soul, supports the decline of the outer world.
James Hillman

PSYCHOTHERAPISTS/PSYCHIATRISTS/COUNSELORS

If you love gossip, you have the chance for greatness as a therapist; if you've always hated it, preferring to concentrate on "bigger things," you will probably be bored in this profession.
George Weinberg

Free people in a free society must never forget or forsake the adage that the expert must be on tap, not on top.
Thomas Szasz

Every therapist in the country could stop practicing and nothing would happen. The patients would find someone else to talk to.
William Glasser

In my mind, learning to be a therapist is not like learning to be a plumber. Plumbers can usually settle for techniques. Therapists need to do more. You don't have to love a pipe to fix it.
Virginia Satir

Only the wounded can heal.
M. Scott Peck

Learn the best, know the best—and then forget everything when you face the patient.
C. G. Jung (Advice to student therapists)

I am skeptical of anybody who profits from another person's suffering.
Jeffrey Moussaieff Masson

People become therapists partially to avoid their own problems.
Rollo May

No one who, like me, conjures up the most evil of those half-tamed demons that inhabit the human breast, and seek to wrestle with them can expect to come through the struggle unscathed.
Sigmund Freud

Anyone who keeps company with counselors knows that, no matter what they may be like with their clients, their personal lives are no freer than the lives of others from pettiness, depression, poor communication, power struggles, anxiety, bad habits, and other difficulties.
Bernie Zilbergeld

It seems fair to say there is no evidence that counselors do better, feel better, or overcome more problems than anyone else.
Bernie Zilbergeld

Thus the analyst's modesty must be no studied pose, but a reflection of the limitation of our knowledge.
Sandor Ferenczi

A therapist is in some ways a substitute parent. He is not simply a guide.
Alexander Lowen I think it only as the therapist views himself as imperfect and flawed that he can see himself as helping another person.
Carl Rogers

I'm generally skeptical when I hear of anybody who has been in therapy for 4 or 5 years—skeptical of the therapist.
William Schutz

He [my therapist] was meddling too much in my private life.
Tennessee Williams (explaining why he quit therapy)

All therapists are vulnerable to mistaking their own world-view for reality. Ironically, we are perhaps even more vulnerable than most other people.
Sheldon Kopp

If you wish to be a good therapist, it is dangerous to have too much of a desire to help people…People who want to help too much can fall into the sentimental trap of love and concern while understanding absolutely nothing.
Mara Selvini Palazzoli

Many therapists see themselves as members of the helping professions engaged in the helping relationship. Beware! Such people are dangerous. If successful, they kill the humanness in their patients by preventing their growth…. The distinction between true support and help is clear: *To do for the other what he is capable of doing for himself insures his not becoming aware that he can stand on his own two feet.*
Robert W. Resnick (From, Chicken Soup is Poison)

The therapist must at all times keep watch over himself, over the way he is reacting to his patient. For we do not react only with our consciousness.
C. G. Jung

At mid-career, we are forced to come to grips with the impossibility of our dreams of clinical omnipotence. We must grudgingly admit that lots of things can't be fixed, made easy, no matter what we do, no matter how skillful we are.
Carol Anderson

The analyst hears not only what is in the words; he also hears what the words do not say. He listens with the "third ear," hearing not only what the patient speaks but also his own inner voices, what emerges from his own unconscious depths.
Theodore Reik

A sensitive person learns, often without being conscious of doing so, to pick up the feelings of the person around him, as a violin string resonates to the vibration of every other musical string in the room.... Every successful lover knows this by "instinct." It is an essential—if not *the* essential—quality of the good therapist.
Rollo May

The technique of treatment must be in yourself.
Alfred Adler

Preparation of the therapist must precede preparation of the patient.
Eric Berne

I am still more frightened by the fearless power in the eyes of my fellow psychiatrists than by the powerless fear in the eyes of their patients.
R. D. Laing

I don't think the therapist does anything except provide the opportunity to think about your problem in a favorable climate.
Milton Erickson

If we ourselves [psychotherapists] know that basic experience of faith and hope, then we can sit with someone who is in despair and know that hope is possible for them.
David Goldblatt

Historically therapists have never been in the forefront of the struggle for social change. It is not in the interest of the profession to create conditions that would lead to the dissolution of psychotherapy.
Jeffrey Moussaieff Masson

I shudder when I think of unsuspecting families and couples going to some of the licensed family therapists I have met, however well meaning the therapist may be.
James Framo

I like the work because one can never become a master of it. The more accomplished one is, the more effortless one's function as a therapist becomes, the more there still remains to be clarified and understood.
Stanley Greben

PSYCHOTHERAPIST—CLIENT/PATIENT RELATIONSHIP

No man is a hero to his wife's psychiatrist.
Eric Berne (Founder of Transactional Analysis)

A caring understanding relationship—made safe by professional ethics and restraint—is the essence of psychotherapy.
Peter R. Breggin

To me the most striking personal discovery of the past decade has been that people respond to my degree of caring more than to my degree of knowing.
C. Gilbert Wrenn

From the standpoint of the consumer, what they want most is not an empathic therapist but rather to get over their suffering…If I were drowning, I would much sooner have somebody who could handle a rowboat and oars and throw a life preserver than somebody who would just stand on shore and suffer for me.
Aaron Beck

We psychotherapists simply cannot cluck with sympathy and exhort patients to struggle resolutely with their problems. We cannot say to them *you* and *your* problems, because our life, our existence, will always

be riveted to death, love to loss, freedom to fear, and growth to separation. We are, all of us, in this together.
Irvin Yalom

The first prerequisite for successful psychotherapy is the respect that the psychiatrist must extend to the mental patient. Such respect can be valid only if the psychiatrist realizes that his patient's difficulties in living are not too different from his own.
Frieda Fromm-Reichmann

What does not interest a patient cannot be forced upon him.
Otto Fenichel

The counselor should not relieve the counselee of suffering, but rather redirect the suffering into constructive channels.
Rollo May

I want you to remember that in the present state of our society, the patient is right, and you are wrong.
H. S. Sullivan (His advice to young psychiatrists)

Now any therapist who wants to be *helpful* is doomed right from the beginning. The patient will do anything to make the therapist feel inadequate, because he has to have his compensation for needing him.
Fritz Perls

The more active and forceful the therapist (even if ostensibly in the service of helping the patient assume responsibility), the more is the patient infantilized.
Irvin Yalom

People already have what they need to grow and the therapist's task is to enable patients to utilize their own resources.
Virginia Satir (Pioneer in Family Therapy)

Our primary material is always the poetry and artistry in people.
Peggy Papp

The therapist's *raison d'être* is to be midwife to the birth of the patient's yet unlived life.
Irvin Yalom

As a therapist I am no more a "reinforcing machine" than my patient is a "talking pigeon."
R. A. Schonbar

Somehow, I feel that orthodox therapists (we might call them Rogerian, Freudian, or even Skinnerian technicians) are more concerned to verify their respective dogmas than to know and respond to their patients as individual persons. Techniques treat with categories and fictions. Therapy proceeds through honest responses to this very person by this very person.
Sidney Jourard

Insofar as you can truly build a bridge of empathy to a person, to that extent he is not psychotic.
Heinz Kohut

The recovery of many schizophrenics and schizoid personalities, for example, depends upon the psychotherapist's freedom from convention and prejudice. These patients cannot and should not be asked to accept guidance toward a conventional adjustment to the customary requirements of our culture, much less to what the individual therapist personally considers these requirements to be.
Frieda Fromm-Reichmann

The helper who is tense and tight will almost inevitably infect his client with his own malaise.
Gerald Egan

If therapy is a voyage of self-discovery, it should be conducted by a guide who has personally made this voyage. A therapist cannot help patients advance beyond the point where he or she has personally gone.
Alexander Lowen

Many things—a simple group exercise, a few minutes of deep reflection, a work of art, a sermon, a personal crisis, a loss—remind us that our deepest wants can never be fulfilled: our wants for youth, for a halt to

aging, for the return of vanished ones, for eternal love, protection, significance, for immortality itself. It is when these unattainable wants come to dominate our lives that we turn for help to family, to friends, to religion—sometimes to psychotherapists.
Irvin Yalom

It is probably true that many of us in the mental health professions, through dint of effort and sense of duty, attend better to our patients than to people in the rest of our lives, but with them, too we suffer from the inability really to listen fully and see clearly.
John B. Enright

The therapist is able to be where he himself is and where the patient is; the patient cannot be but where he is.
Martin Buber

The therapist must become a fellow traveler with his patient.
R. D. Laing

Face it, when a patient pays a therapist, all he's doing is buying a friend.
William Glasser

What we need are more kindly friends and fewer professionals.
Jeffrey Moussaieff Masson

In the best of cases the analyst makes a colossal effort to overcome his yawning boredom and behave in a friendly and compassionate manner. Were we to encourage our patients to real freedom [of expression], and to overcome their anxiety and embarrassment toward us, we would soon learn that patients at some level are actually acutely aware of all our real feelings and thoughts.
Sándor Ferenczi

The integrity of the family must be respected. They must write their own destiny. In the same sense that the individual has a right to suicide, the family has the right to self-destruct. The therapist may not, and does not, have the power to mold their system to his will. He's their coach, but he's not playing on the team.
Carl Whitaker

It is not the therapist who discovers and announces the truth, it is the patient who ultimately can confirm, by her won responses, that which is true for her.
Stanley Greben

I always regard myself as the advocate of the child in my patients; whatever they may tell me, I take their side completely…I consciously identify with the mute child in the patient.
Alice Miller

Every patient has the right to be regarded and treated, as an abused and unhappy child.
Sándor Ferenczi

Medicines cure diseases but only doctors can cure patients.
C. G. Jung

The repressed memory is like a noisy intruder being thrown out of the concert hall. You can throw him out, but he will bang on the door and continue to disturb the concert. The analyst opens the door and says. "If you promise to behave yourself, you can come back in."
Theodore Reik

Clinicians, most of whom are men, all too often treat their patients, most of whom are women, as 'wives' and 'daughters,' rather than as people: treat them as if female misery, by biological definition, exists outside the realm of what is considered human or adult.
Phyllis Chesler

The doctor who joins his patient on the couch helps her about as much as the master who joins his maid in the linen closet.
Phyllis Chesler

Free association: the term a psychoanalyst uses to register approval of the patient who talks about what the analyst wants him to talk about.
Thomas Szasz

No doubt fate would find it easier than I do to relieve you of your illness. But you will be able to convince yourself that much will be gained

if we succeed in transforming your hysterical misery into common unhappiness.
Sigmund Freud

PSYCHOTHERAPEUTIC TECHNIQUES/ APPROACHES/THEORIES

Psychoanalysis is the disease it purports to cure.
Karl Kraus

Psychoanalysis is like music lessons, for 5 years you do not notice any progress and suddenly you can play the piano.
Woody Allen

Psychoanalysis makes quite simple people feel they're complex.
S. N. Behrman

It is no exaggeration to say that psychoanalysis; much like psychiatry in general, was founded on the betrayal of women and children.
Peter R. Breggin

Of course Behaviorism works. So does torture.
W. H. Auden

If one wishes to do effective therapy with mad people, it is best simply to abandon psychodynamic theory.
Jay Haley

The various Behaviorisms all seem to generate inexorably such a passive image of a helpless man, one who has little to say about his own fate.
Abraham Maslow.

Psychoanalysis once worked at the roots of life. The fact that it did not become conscious of its social nature was the main factor in its catastrophic decline.
Wilhelm Reich

Psychoanalysis, with its emphasis on the individual and on intrapsychic phenomena as separate from their context, has encouraged the develop-

ment of a diagnostic system and models of delivery of services which do not take into account the complexity of peoples' lives.
Salvatore Minuchin

While insight was very helpful to Freud the scientist (and thus informs us all), the patient needs more.
Augustus Napier

Psychoanalysis is not concerned with the real world, nor with the child's or the adult's adaptation to the real world, nor with sickness nor health, nor virtue nor vice. It is concerned simply and solely with the imaginings of the childish mind, the phantasied pleasures and the dreaded retributions.
Melanie Klein

Our profession has too long operated on the belief that it was doing a good job for the public. It is time that we forget about our exaggerated claims, about the theories of *Sigmund Freud* and our mystical shibboleths of the Unconscious and start doing the solid research necessary for a profession with integrity.
Arthur K. Shapiro

I disagree with manipulative approaches to therapy; to assume that one person can be in charge of another's life is a dangerous philosophy.
Carl Rogers

To the extent that a behaviorist point of view in psychology is leading us toward a disregard of the person, toward treating persons primarily as manipulable objects, toward control of the person by shaping his behavior without his participant choice, or toward minimizing the significance of the subjective—to that extent I question it very deeply. My experience leads me to say that such a point of view is going against one of the strongest undercurrents of modern life, and is taking us down a pathway with destructive consequences.
Carl Rogers (In a debate with B. F. Skinner in 1956)

All that is required of counselors is being real. The only value is authenticity. To achieve this, counselors must be willing to forsake all theories about how a good counselor should respond.
Len Bergantino

Theorizing, if not theory, is treacherous. Woven initially out of our fantasies, theories can become powerful, dominant controlling shackles.
Walter Kempler

My theory is that all theories are bad except for the beginner's game playing, until he gets the courage to give up theories and just live. Because it has been known for many generations that any addiction, any indoctrination tends to be constrictive and constipating.
Carl Whitaker

Understanding theory can change your life more than anything that can happen.
Murray Bowen

Theories in psychology are the very devil. It is true that we need certain points of view for orienting and heuristic value; but they should always be regarded as mere auxiliary concepts that can be laid aside any time.
C. G. Jung

The current state of psychological knowledge does not permit the development of an accurate theory of human functioning.
Arnold Lazarus

Theory is simply the best we can do to date to conceptualize the experiences our patients present to us.
Harry Guntrip

To try to determine by scientific analysis how much better or worse, let us say, gestalt therapy is than transactional analysis is in many ways equivalent to attempting to determine by the same means the relative merits of Cole Porter and Richard Rogers. To ask the question is to reveal its absurdity.
Jerome Frank

The greater freedom from dogmatic beliefs, which I found in this country, alleviated the obligation of taking psychoanalytical theories for granted, and gave me the courage to proceed along the lines which I considered right.
Karen Horney

In the end, it is all in the listening. The rest will follow in more directions than you and I can imagine.
Robert Langs

And I do wish that Rogerian therapists, Gestalt therapists, transactional analysts, group analysts, and all the other offspring of various theories would recognize that not one of them really recognizes that psychotherapy for person #1 is not psychotherapy for person #2.
Milton Erickson

All three of these theoretical orientations [Freudian or traditionalist, behaviorist, and humanist] eclipse major portions of reality: the traditionalists and humanists (each in different ways) deny the impact of social reality, while the behaviorists deny the impact of consciousness.
Miriam Greenspan

Playing the sage and behaving like a guru is endemic to family therapy. Indeed it is prescribed in the standard textbooks in the field.
Jeffrey Moussaieff Masson

I think family therapy is a field with many people who do not shy away from the pleasure of playing to audiences and being charismatic. This is a field with a lot of very narcissistic people who enjoy that game.
Salvatore Minuchin

What matters is not a technique or therapeutic approach as such, be it drug treatment or shock treatment, but the spirit in which it is being carried out.
Viktor Frankl

Gestalt therapy is being in touch with the obvious.
Fritz Perls

R

RANK, OTTO (1884–1939)

Otto Rank was born Otto Rosenfeld on April 22, 1884. At the age of nineteen he changed his name, partly as a reaction to the poor relationship he had with his father. Alfred Adler, his family doctor, introduced him to Freud who was impressed by one of Rank's manuscripts. He later broke with Freud and developed his own ap-proach that rejected therapy by technique and interpretation of the past, and emphasizing the experiencing of the present in the therapeutic situation. He had a strong influence on the thinking of Carl Rogers.

If with respect to Freud one can say, "The unexamined life is not worth living," then on behalf of Rank one can say, "The uncreative life is not worth living."
E. James Lieberman

If Freud embodies the scientific attitude, the attitude of the student and experimenter who puts humanity outside of himself in order to observe and analyze objectively, Rank stands at the opposite pole, carrying into the field of psychotherapy the vision and scope of the artist, the man who includes within himself the opposition science sets up, who is at once doctor and patient, experimenter and subject, scholar and healer, helper and helped.
Jessie Taft

Rank brought the human relationship directly into his office. He influenced analysts to take seriously the actual present interaction between therapist and patient...Rank's contributions opened the way for *encounter* to become accepted as a deep therapeutic agent.
Erving Polster

...how deep was his gift, how vivid his human experience?...He did have sorrows, profound depressions, disappointments, frustrations, but he never became bitter or cynical. His faith never died, nor his capacity to feel, to respond.
Anais Nin (author)

But Rank, with his breadth of learning in literature, his fascination with mythology, and eventually his defection from the mechanistic science of psychoanalysis, had a great deal in common with Jung, although he would hardly have admitted it. After years of seeing Jung and Adler as defectors, he was not likely to turn suddenly and recognize a brother.
John Conger

Rank, in a dramatic fashion,…developed psychotic manifestations that revealed themselves in, among other ways, a turning away from Freud and his doctrines.
Ernest Jones

The little fellow always tried to set the old gentleman [Freud] against me!
Alfred Adler

REALITY/*Fantasy*

Sometimes a cigar is just a cigar.
Sigmund Freud

All therapists are vulnerable to mistaking their own world-view for reality. Ironically, we are perhaps even more vulnerable than most other people.
Sheldon Kopp

The belief that one's own view of reality is the only reality is the most dangerous of all delusions.
Paul Watzlawick

Why is this idea of another reality so threatening to psychologists? I believe it is because we are one of the most insecure of sciences. We do not *dare* to investigate the mysterious.
Carl Rogers

We may lay it down that a happy person never phantasies, only an unsatisfied one. The motive forces of phantasies are unsatisfied wishes, and every single phantasy is the fulfillment of a wish, a correction of an unsatisfying reality.
Sigmund Freud

If we accept as a basic fact of all human life that we live in separate realities; if we can see those differing realities as the most promising resource for learning in all the history of the world; if we can live together in order to learn from one another without fear; if we can do all this, then a new age could be dawning.
Carl Rogers

We see the shadows but take them for the substance.
R. D. Laing

Attempts to determine reality for another person, to *give* meaning to another's experience, *deny* the self. These other-directed meanings cannot be assimilated.
Clark Moustakas

There is not one space and time only, but as many spaces and times as there are subjects.
Ludwig Binswanger

REICH, WILHELM (1897–1957)

Wilhelm Reich was among the first to focus on the role of the body in psychological disorders, and influenced Fritz Perls, Alexander Lowen and other body based therapists who draw on his belief that trauma is expressed in tense muscles and disturbed breathing. Reich's life is probably the most tragic of all the leading psychotherapists. He was born the eldest of two sons of a Jewish family in what is now Romania. His father was strict and hot-tempered, and beat him often for even the slightest infraction. His mother was often away for medical treatment at spas. He learned about sex at an early age from the farm animals and farmhands. By the age of eleven he claimed to be having daily intercourse with the family cook. When he was twelve years old he discovered his mother having an affair with his tutor, and informed his father. As punishment his father mentally and physically abused his mother for almost a year until she finally succeeded in committing suicide. Reich's father died of tuberculosis a few years later. In another tragic incident one of his female patients, Lore Kahn, who he became sexually involved with also committed suicide. He fell in love with another patient, Annie Pink. Her family placed pressure on Reich to marry her, and Reich finally capitulated perhaps out of fear of another tragedy. The marriage lasted ten years. There were two children, one whom he named after Lore Kahn.

Reich graduated from medical school in Vienna, and was part of the Vienna Psychoanalytic Society. He became interested in the psychological contents of mental disorders, and the ways these disorders manifested themselves physically. He looked beyond the patient's presenting symptoms to what he called the "character armor," or the person's characteristic way of warding off anxiety.
Reich was also a Marxist, and criticized Freud's avoidance of social factors in human development. He attempted to synthesize the works of Freud and Marx, but alienated many people in the process. He was expelled from the Communist Party, the International Psychoanalytic Association, and Norway where he tried to settle. He eventually found his way to America where he developed and marketed an "orgone accumulator" which he claimed would increase the life energy. The FDA prosecuted him for fraud, and he was ordered to cease marketing his accumulators, and to destroy them. In 1955 he was tried and convicted for contempt of the FDA injunction, and sent to jail for two years. Eight months later he was found dead in his jail cell.

Reich, was the first man I trusted.
Fritz Perls (Perls was analyzed by Reich)

Reich was the one who really developed [the new therapy] in understanding the body as a reflection of the personality. That insight has been internalized into a lot of therapies that I know of.
William Schutz

He had brilliant ideas, a cosmic perspective, and a holistic and dynamic worldview that far surpassed the science of his time and was not appreciated by his contemporaries.
Fritjof Capra

Reich was a disturbed man on some level, but he was a genius on another.... At the end of his life, he went off, no question about it. But that happens to a lot of geniuses, and doesn't reflect upon their work. In my opinion it sometimes takes a crazy man to see the insanity in our culture.
Alexander Lowen

While American psychiatry struggled to "adjust" the individual to society, it could hardly be receptive to Reich's Marxist version of Freudian analysis, the goal of which was to adjust the society to the needs of the individual. Reich the "red," like Reich the "quack" had failed to grasp

the higher mysteries of ego reinforcement, behaviorism, and electric shock. So much the worse for Reich.
Andrew Feenberg

We have here a Dr. Reich, a worthy but impetuous young man, passionately devoted to his hobbyhorse, who now salutes in the genital orgasm the antidote to every neurosis.
Sigmund Freud 1928 (In a letter to Lou Andreas-Salomé)

Of course Reich was wrong as later developments showed...Reich was misled because at his time the conservatives had a strict sexual morality and he concluded from this that sexual liberty would lead to an anticonservative revolutionary attitude.
Erich Fromm

Wilhelm was right in emphasizing the roots of fascism in instinctual repression; he was wrong when he saw the mainsprings for the defeat of fascism in sexual liberation.
Herbert Marcuse

So if anyone asks me about *Wilhelm Reich*, for example, I'd say "He was psychotic all his life," which he was, and that some of his writings have some nauseating shit in them.
Albert Ellis

Because of what Reich found, demonstrated and taught, the great gap between religion and science, body and spirit, was narrowed. A fresh way out of man's prison appeared through the fog.... He touched the heart of something; maybe he touched the vibration of life. Perhaps it was because he touched something so precious, so very sensitive, so long forgotten, that he was reviled, slandered and castigated from every side. He died in prison, the victim of what he had labeled the Emotional Plague—man's terror of living.
James Wyckoff

RELATIONSHIPS

In our differences we grow; in our sameness we connect.
Virginia Satir (Pioneer in Family Therapy)

In our civilization, men are afraid that they will not be men enough and women are afraid that they might be considered only women.
Theodore Reik

Jealousy characterizes the relationship in which one seeks more power than love.
Rollo May

Sometimes it seems to me that in this absurdly random life there is some inherent justice in the outcome of personal relationships. In the long run, we get no more than we have been willing to risk giving.
Sheldon Kopp

Self-disclosure between men reduces the mystery that one man is for another.
Sidney Jourard

Most married couples conduct themselves as if each party were afraid that the other one could see it was the weaker.
Alfred Adler

The only way you can make a marriage work is as free, independent people. It needs to be based on the good feelings that you have for each other, not on need.
Alexander Lowen

Everyone is deeply interested in maintaining the faults of his partner.
Rudolf Dreikurs

One, after all, does not *find* a relationship; one forms a relationship.
Irvin Yalom

It is from one to another that the heavenly bread of self-being is passed.
Martin Buber

Contact is the appreciation of differences.
Fritz Perls

We need relations, the sharedness of being. Trying to be totally self-sufficient is a perversion.
James Bugental

To make peace between the sexes, make peace within the person.
Abraham Maslow

To make friends with some portion of the outside world, it is well to make friends with that part of it which is within yourself.
Abraham Maslow

All relationships are temporary, but it is so terribly hard with my wife, my kids, my friends, the people whom I love most, it's so terribly hard to remember that we have so little time. We stall, kid ourselves, promise that we will deal with things some time soon. Not only are there many things that we never get around to dealing with, but even when we do, there is so damn much waste in the process, so much unnecessary distance between ourselves and those with whom we try to make a life.
Sheldon Kopp

Helping women, treating them, bestowing gifts—these are done much more for the donor's sake, as assertions of his superiority.
Rudolf Dreikurs

Therapy pushes the relationship issues, but what intensifies those issues is that we don't have (a) satisfactory work or (b), even m ore important perhaps, we don't have a satisfactory political community.
James Hillman

A meeting of two: eye to eye, face to face.
And when you are near I will tear your eyes out
And place them instead of mine,
And you will tear my eyes out
And will place them instead of yours.
Then I will look at you with your eyes
And you will look at me with mine.
Jacob L. Moreno

RELIGION

Religion is comparable to a childhood neurosis.
Sigmund Freud

When a man is freed of religion, he has a better chance to live a normal and wholesome life.
Sigmund Freud

I believe exactly as much in religious commitment—and the prayer, devotion, and ritual that normally accompany it—as I do in commitment to Santa Claus and my fairy godmother.
Albert Ellis

I oppose religiosity, which I have defined as a dogmatic, fanatical belief in theological religion (e.g., Christianity) *and* in secular religion (e.g., fascism and Freudianism).
Albert Ellis

Formerly, when religion was strong and science weak, men mistook magic for medicine; now, when science is strong and religion weak, men mistake medicine for magic.
Thomas Szasz

The appeal of every religion is the feeling of community it engenders. A religious person feels himself part of a community of man, to belong to the community of nature, and to participate in the community of God or the universe. And every person who feels this way is a religious person, whether or not he is a member of a religious group.
Alexander Lowen

It is my contention that pietistic theists and religionists—virtually all people imbued with intense religiosity and fanaticism—are emotionally disturbed: usually neurotic but sometimes psychotic. For they strongly and rigidly believe in the same kinds of profound irrationalities, abolutistic musts, and unconditional necessities in which seriously disturbed people powerfully believe.
Albert Ellis

I think Ellis sees religion as a personally oppressive force. I do not see that strong religionists are any worse off than atheists in terms of depression and anxiety. In some cases they are better off. The Catholics, for example, have a much lower suicide rate in general than non-Catholics.
David Burns

A religion, even if it calls itself the religion of love, must be hard and unloving to those who do not belong to it. Fundamentally, every religion is a religion of love for those whom it embraces, while cruelty and intolerance towards those who do not belong to it are natural to every religion.
Sigmund Freud

If one attempts to assign to religion its place in man's evolution, it seems not so much to be a lasting acquisition, as a parallel to the neurosis which the civilized individual must pass through on his way from childhood to maturity.
Sigmund Freud

Hatred for Judaism is at bottom hatred for Christianity.
Sigmund Freud

RESPONSIBILITY

Two wrongs don't make a right, but they make a good excuse.
Thomas Szasz

Genuine responsibility exists only where there is real responding.
Martin Buber

Blaming others, or outside conditions for one's own misbehavior may be the child's privilege; if an adult denies responsibility for his actions, it is another step towards personality disintegration.
Bruno Bettelheim

The proverb warns that, 'You should not bite the hand that feeds you.' But maybe you should, if it prevents you from feeding yourself.
Thomas Szasz

Once we accept responsibility for choosing our lives, everything is different. We have the power. We decide. We are in control.
William Schutz

Irresponsible people always seeking to gain happiness without assuming responsibility, find only brief periods of joy, but not the deep-seated satisfaction, which accompanies responsible behavior.
William Glasser

And the question mark is the hook of a demand. Every time you refuse to answer a question you help the other person to develop his own resources.
Fritz Perls

I feel a sense of historical urgency, as well as an increased awareness of the responsibility of the psychologist. This is a responsibility to the human race, and it should give the psychologist a sense of mission and a weight of duty beyond those of other scientists.
Abraham Maslow

REWARD

The unlimited devotion of a parent or the lifelong dedication to a cause cannot be paid for or rewarded, it can only be accepted and need not even be recognized.
Laura Perls

ROGERS, CARL (1902–1987)

In the 1940's Rogers originated and founded an alternative non-directive method to psychotherapy which challenged established therapeutic procedures and assumptions. The approach, which came to be known as client centered therapy and later person centered therapy, caused a furor in the psychotherapeutic community. Rogers originated and developed the prevailing humanistic trend in psychology, pioneered in psychotherapy research, and influenced all the helping professions.

Rogers began applying his approach to group work including therapy and encounter groups. He conducted workshops and seminars around the world for business and political leaders, educators, psychotherapists and others.

When he was 80 he decided to devote the rest of his life to working toward world peace. He traveled to such places as Northern Ireland, South Africa, Hungary, Brazil, and the Soviet Union working with people from conflicting political factions in trying to resolve conflicts. He remained active to just a few days before his death.

ROGERS ON HIMSELF

I must constantly resist the temptation to rush in and fix things.

Writing is my way of communicating with a world to which, in a very real sense, I feel I do not quite belong.

The degree to which I can create relationships which facilitate the growth of others as separate persons is a measure of the growth I have achieved for myself.

Many people are not aware that I am a tease and that I can be very tenacious and tough, almost obstinate. I have often said that those who think I am always gentle should get into a fight with me, because they would find out quite differently.

OTHERS ON ROGERS

He felt somehow that the solutions to problems rested within the individual and that the therapist should bring them out, but I felt people are really changed by the changing world they live in.
    B.F. Skinner

Certain humanistic notions that might apply to normal people such as fulfillment and being free of cultural bondage are simply not relevant to the abnormal states. Rogers has made an enormous contribution and influenced many contemporary therapists, including me. But his notion regarding normal development simply did not seem to apply to abnormal situations.
Aaron Beck

What Rogers boasts of so proudly as self-actualization may be but the pathology of a culture whose members are frightened at being cut off from past traditions and rush pell-mell into the future, as if they were animals in stampede.
Marshall C. Lowe

Rogers claims that the therapist must possess no moralistic or judgmental attitude whatsoever, it is interesting that in every single case he describes as successful the client always attaches himself to goals, or accepts roles that would meet the hearty approval of any Methodist minister.
Arnold W. Green

I also spent a summer at the University of Chicago under Dr. *Carl Rogers* and his students. He was a man whose very therapeutic system was based on respect for, and trust in the self of another. During that summer I experienced what it meant to have a "thou-thou" relationship with others.
Everett Shostorm

Reading Rogers is such a bland experience that I found myself recalling the old adage that psychotherapy is the process whereby the bland teach the unbland to be bland. This reaction points to something lacking in Rogers and his writings, and that is sensitivity to people's real suffering.
Jeffrey Moussaieff Masson

…a man whose cumulative effect on society has made him one of the most important social revolutionaries of our time.
Richard Farson

Roger's contributions are so pervasive and have become so ingrained in our thinking and practice that we no longer consider many of them "Rogerian." Also, it is interesting to see that Roger's model has become

something of a standard against which other, more recently popular models are compared.
Rodney K. Goodyear

He's probably second only to Freud in many people's impression in terms of his impact on the whole field of psychology and psychotherapy.
David Malcolm

Carl R. Rogers is one of the few who are totally American who have had a pervasive impact on the field of psychotherapy. Consistently he advances his conviction that human beings are essentially good and to be trusted, that they have the potential to heal themselves, and that honest relationships are the major force for change and betterment in human affairs. In his own life, as well, this man has sought to live what he taught so well to so many.
James Bugental

He cared about each person—but not about the institutions. He did not care about appearances, roles, class, credentials, or positions, and he doubted every authority including his own.
Eugene T. Gendlin

Carl Rogers has pioneered once again in trying to apply person-centered psychology to political and social situations that are highly volatile and often dangerous. His results are impressive and indicate that something can indeed be done to help change people's negative feelings toward each other and toward grim political realities.
Albert Ellis

Whether or not those forces in civilization which aim to give each person dignity, respect and control over his or her life are ultimately triumphant, Rogers will have taken a stand and played a part in the outcome.
Howard Kirchenbaum

S

SATIR, VIRGINIA (1916–1988)

Virginia Satir was the founder of the school of Conjoint Family Therapy, and a major figure in the field of marital and family therapy. She was often referred to as the "Columbus of Family Therapy" because she traveled widely presenting workshops and delivering papers. She was active, productive, and energetic to the end of her career when she died of cancer.

Virginia, you have my love and my unstinted admiration. In many respects we are alike. Restless Gypsy. Greedy for success and recognition. Not willing to settle for mediocrity. You are a big woman with a big heart. Eager to learn. Fantasy for things to come. Your greatest asset is that you make people listen. You suffer, like me, from intellectual systematitis, but what you think and what you do don't quite come together.
Fritz Perls

Like a surgeon, she goes to areas of disconnectedness and tries to create different ways of contacting. But I think humans are complex organisms. Besides the positive affects—intimacy, cooperation, love, the need to be close and belong—there is also the wish to be separate. There is anger, and competitiveness, and jockeying for power. I think her therapy, focused primarily on repairing the breakages of intimacy, is a very partial view.
Salvatore Minuchin

SCIENCE

Science can be the religion of the non-religious, the poetry of the non-poet, the art of the man who cannot paint, the humor of the serious man, and the love-making of the inhibited and shy man. Not only does science begin in wonder, it also ends in wonder.
Abraham Maslow

I detest much of the theory and practice of natural science and biology.
R. D. Laing

SECRETS

All personal secrets have the effect of sin or guilt.
C. G. Jung

SELF-AFFIRMATION/SELF-ACCEPTANCE

Affirming one's own being creates the values of life.
Rollo May

If you feel comfortable in yourself, you don't love yourself and you don't hate yourself, you just live.
Fritz Perls

SELF-BETRAYAL

The serious thing for each person to recognize vividly and poignantly, each for himself, is that every falling away from species—virtue, every crime against one's own nature, every evil act, every one without exception records itself in our unconscious and makes us despise ourselves.
Abraham Maslow

The ultimate consequence of betrayal of the self is alienation and inauthenticity.
Clark Moustakas

SELF-DECEPTION

It is well to remember that academicians and professionals are as prone to self-deception as anyone else.
Jerome Frank

SELF-DISCIPLINE

Only to the self-disciplined person can one say, "Do as you will, and it will probably be all right."
Abraham Maslow

SELF-KNOWLEDGE/SELF-UNDERSTANDING

Everything that irritates us about others can lead us to an understanding of ourselves.
C. G. Jung

One is always in the dark about one's own personality. One needs others to get to know oneself.
C. G. Jung

Many problems simply disappear; many others are easily solved by knowing what is in conformity with one's own nature, what is suitable and right.
Abraham Maslow

Knowledge of one's own deep nature is also simultaneously knowledge of human nature in general.
Abraham Maslow

The organism knows all. We know very little.
Fritz Perls

This is all very well. But if organisms are self-regulating, why then do we need all of these techniques to help us regulate ourselves? If the body really is so "wise," shouldn't it be able to get along fine on its own?
Edwin Schur

Is it sufficient that you have learned to drive the car, or shall we look and see what is under the hood? Most people go through life without ever knowing.
June Singer

SEX

The sexual drive is nothing but the motor memory of previously experienced pleasure.
Wilhelm Reich

In the orgasm the living organism is nothing but a part of pulsating nature
Wilhelm Reich

Men generally are not candid in sexual matters. They do not show their sexuality freely, but they wear a thick overcoat—a fabric of lies—to conceal it, as though it were bad weather in the world of sex.
Sigmund Freud

Sexual potency, force, and drive of a human being are to some extent determined by inheritance and chemistry. Incredible as it may seem, they are even more strongly influenced by the script decisions he makes in early childhood and by the parental programming that brings about those decisions. Thus not only the authority and frequency of his sexual activities throughout his whole lifetime, but also his ability and readiness to love are to a large extent already decided at the age of six.
Eric Berne

SHAME

Doubt is the brother of shame.
Erik Erikson

I think…we've lost shame…We've lost our shame in relation to the world, the shame of being wrong, of messing up the world.
James Hillman

SKINNER, BURRHUS FREDERIC (1904–1990)

Burrhus Frederic Skinner, was one of the leading figures in the school of behavioral psychology. After World War II Skinner came to fame by publishing an article in the <u>Ladies Home Journal</u> describing an "air-crib" he had designed and built for his youngest daughter in order to provide her with a comfortable,

stimulating, optimum environment. The controversial crib received much attention and came to be known as a "Skinner box." He posited that human beings are externally controlled, and that freedom as an internal psychological phenomenon, is a result of external conditioning. In 1948 he wrote his controversial book, Walden Two *in which he extrapolated behaviorist principles to solving contemporary social issues. The book has sold well over a million copies. Skinner received many honors and awards, and was prolific throughout his life.*

SKINNER ON HIMSELF

The organism whose behavior I observed most closely was myself.
  (Skinner was known to keep charts of his own behavior and present himself with rewards for achievements.)

I have said that "I was taught to fear God, the police, and what people will think," and traces of that childhood survive. I have never cared much about clothing, but I would never appear at a scientific meeting in an informal jacket or sweater. Thoreau said of Emerson that he would rather have walked down the street with a broken leg than a broken pantleg, and I am afraid I am rather like that.

I do not admire myself as a person. My successes do not override my shortcomings. When I played the saxophone in dance orchestras, I read the notes; I could never break free as jazz required. I found it almost impossible to paint nonrepresentationally. William Sewell, the sculptor who made the satirical ceramic statue of me, once told me I would "have to be psychoanalyzed" if I were ever to paint well.

I do not like being an eponym.

I would bury my children rather than my books. But I would give the same answer with respect to myself. If some Mephistopheles offered me a wholly new life on condition that all records and effects of my present life be destroyed, I should refuse.

I never answer any of my critics. I generally don't even read them. There are better things to do with my time than clear up their misunderstanding.

It [*Walden Two*] gives young people a chance to speculate about government and political behavior in a nonpolitical way. I mean, what else can a young man do if he wants to dream about a better world—become a Republican?

(*Skinner explaining the popularity of his novel about a utopian society based on the scientific control of human behavior.*)

As the senses grow dull, the stimulating environment becomes less clear. When reinforcing consequences no longer follow, we are bored, discouraged, and depressed.... Our environment is no longer maintaining strong behavior.

(*explanation of his declining powers in his later years*)

OTHERS ON SKINNER

I would like to say I have acquired an increasing respect for Dr. Skinner the person, his sincerity, gentleness, his wit, his wide scholarly interests, and the honesty with which he is trying to face the implications of the directions in which the behavioral sciences are taking us. I have learned deeply from him, both in the past and during these meetings. [*Rogers and Skinner met for several debates.*] I have often felt and would like to say that I think he is the one person in the behavioral stream of psychology who has had a highly significant impact on our society and on our culture, and I respect his work.
   Carl Rogers

In contrast to *B. F. Skinner*, for me, man without freedom and dignity is nothing!
   Everett Shostrom

B. F. Skinner died August 18, 1990. This leads to the question, who, or what died? Was this a person, whose death we might mourn? Or was it a conditioned organism whose capacity to respond to stimuli wore out?
   Thomas Greening

SOCIAL RESPONSIBILITY

Historically therapists have never been in the forefront of the struggle for social change. It is not in the interest of the profession to create conditions that would lead to the dissolution of psychotherapy.
   Jeffrey Moussaieff Masson

The honest psychologist cannot shut his eyes to social conditions which prevent the child from becoming a part of the community and from feeling at home in the world, and which allow him to grow up as though he lived in enemy country. Thus the psychologist must work against nationalism when it is so poorly understood that it harms mankind as a whole; against wars of conquest, revenge, and prestige; against unemployment which plunges people into hopelessness; and against all other obstacles which interfere with the spreading of social interest in the family, the school, and society at large.
Alfred Adler

So, paradoxically, a person who is sincerely and deeply concerned with bettering economic conditions, ending war, or the like, will be most effective if he does not open himself completely, even in the name of compassion, to all these influences, but rather is able to maintain a centered and calm focus on specific issues so he can clearly see what needs to be done.
Roberto Asssagioli

Inner freedom and social interest are not contradictory, but supplementary. Only a free person can truly be a social person, not the victim of social and other pressures, but a free agent as a social being.
Rudolf Dreikers

SOCIETY/CULTURE

When a society is in clash with the universe, once a society transgresses the laws of nature, it loses its survival value, too.
Fritz Perls

When people are out of their minds or disturbed or fucked up…in our culture, in our psychotherapeutic world, we go back to our mothers, fathers and our childhoods…No other culture would do that. It would never be what happened to you with your mother and father forty years ago.
James Hillman

Society attacks early when the individual is helpless.
B. F. Skinner

A society may be termed human in the measure to which its members confirm one another.
Martin Buber

I would like to point out that for the most part modern culture does not, operationally, want persons to be free, in spite of many ideological statements to the contrary.
Carl Rogers

Survival is the only value according to which a culture is eventually to be judged, and any practice that furthers survival has survival value by definition.
B. F. Skinner

The good society is, thus, the one which gives the greatest freedom to its people—freedom defined not negatively and defensively, but positively, as the opportunity to realize ever greater human values.
Rollo May

SPIRITUALITY

Nothing is more repulsive than a furtively prurient spirituality; it is just as unsavory as gross sensuality.
C. G. Jung

What we really have in common with our remote ancestors is a *spiritual*, not a primitive self, and this we cannot afford to admit because we pride ourselves on living on a purely rational plane.
Otto Rank

SPORT

Sport is imposing order on what was chaos.
Anthony Storr

SUCCESS

Six essential qualities that are the key to success: Sincerity, personal integrity, humility, courtesy, wisdom, charity.
William Menninger

If a person succeeds in giving and receiving love, and can do so with some consistency throughout his life, he is to some degree a success.
William Glasser

SUICIDE

This fundamental possibility of choosing suicide, this liberty of man to decide whether he shall be at all, distinguishes his being from all other kinds of being and marks its contrast with the mode of being of animals.
Viktor Frankl

SULLIVAN, HARRY STACK (1892–1949)

Harry Stack Sullivan was the founder of the interpersonal approach to psychotherapy. He rejected most of Freud's theory of psychosexual development. He believed that personality is shaped by social factors such as parental influence, and therefore emphasized the individual's interpersonal situation, both real and symbolic.
Sullivan chose to work mainly with schizophrenics. His method was to treat each patient as a person rather than a label.

But his own life was not a therapeutic success story. He had psychotic episodes throughout his life, was an alcoholic, irresponsible in his handling of money, cruel toward his students, extremely secretive about the details of his life, and unable fully to accept his homosexual inclinations or to change them. He often despaired of his inability to achieve a "relationship of love."
Bernie Zilbergeld

Sullivan's argument was part of his whole stand which insisted that Freud overemphasized the biological and instinctive giving too little attention to the experiential and social. It is an interesting footnote that Sullivan himself is often described as cold and aloof, relatively unresponsive.
James Bugental

We could look at the work of *Harry Stack Sullivan* which reflects a very brilliant therapist and theorist; yet people who knew him as an individual describe him as being withdrawn and passive—rather schizoid. Nevertheless he developed a tremendous ability to deal with schizophrenic patients and pioneered in their therapy with them.
Richard I. Evans

SURVIVAL

Survival today depends on reducing, controlling, channeling, and redirecting the drive for power and the impulse of violence and fostering countervailing drives toward fellowship and community.
Jerome Frank

THOMAS SZASZ (1920)

Thomas Szasz is probably one of the most controversial psychiatrists. He is a prolific author having written hundreds of articles, and numerous books, his most noted being <u>The Myth of Mental Illness</u>. He has been an outspoken critic of the medical model applied to mental health issues. He was born in Budapest, Hungary, the younger of two sons of Julius and Lily Szasz. His father was an affluent landowner. After Hitler's invasion of Austria, he and his family moved to the United States where he enrolled in the University of Cincinnati and earned a B.A. degree in Physics. His interests then changed and he decided to pursue a medical degree which he received in 1944 graduating at the top of his class at the University of Cincinnati. He was trained in psychoanalysis at the Chicago Institute for Psychoanalysis, where he became a member of the staff.

Szasz has argued that literal illnesses are bodily illnesses and that so-called mental illnesses are either bodily diseases with mental symptoms or metaphorical diseases.

Like many people who are violent in print, he is personally charming, quiet, sober, conventionally dressed, and a model citizen.
 Karl Sabbagh

Szasz's professed apolitical concern with individual rights can be (and has been) put to conservative uses. His opposition to state uses of psychiatry shades uneasily into condemnation of almost all state action aimed at "helping" people.
 Edwin Schur

Thomas Szasz has helped to dispel some naiveté about institutional treatment, but his fundamental premise is erroneous and regressive, denying the valid services psychiatry can offer to a society much in need. To serve, we risk the abuse of our powers; to avoid that risk is not to serve at all.
 Richard R. Parlour

Quite probably he has done more than any other man to alert the American public to the potential dangers of an excessively psychiatrized society.
 Edwin Schur

T

TORTURE

The healthy man does not torture others—generally it is the tortured who turn into torturers.
C. G. Jung

TRADITIONS

Today we live in an age of crumbling and vanishing traditions.
Viktor Frankl

TRANSITION

When an age is in throes of profound transition, the first thing to disintegrate is language.
Rollo May

TRUST

Let us dare, despite all, to trust.
Martin Buber

TRUTH

The truth is often a terrible weapon of aggression. It is possible to lie, and even to murder, with the truth.
Alfred Adler

Truth has disappeared.
R. D. Laing

The Truth does *not* make people free. Facts do *not* change attitudes.
Sheldon Kopp

I've decided that about 80 or 90 percent of all problems in organizations are problems of not telling the truth.
William Schutz

TYRANNY

The more absolute the tyranny, the more debilitated the subject, the more tempting to him to "regain" strength by becoming part of the tyranny and thus enjoy its power.
Bruno Bettelheim (Psychoanalyst)

U-V

UNDERSTANDING

If one does not understand a person, one tends to regard him as a fool.
C. G. Jung

UNIQUENESS

Every individual embodies and contains a uniqueness, a reality that makes him unlike any other person or thing. To maintain this uniqueness in the face of threats and pressures, in times of shifting patterns and moods, is the ultimate challenge of responsibility of every man.
Clark Moustakas

Every person born into this world represents something new, something that never existed before, something original and unique…Every single man is a new thing in the world and is called upon to fulfill his particularity in this world.
Martin Buber

UNIVERSE

The universe was a vast machine yesterday; it is a hologram today. Who knows what intellectual rattle we'll be shaking tomorrow.
R. D. Laing

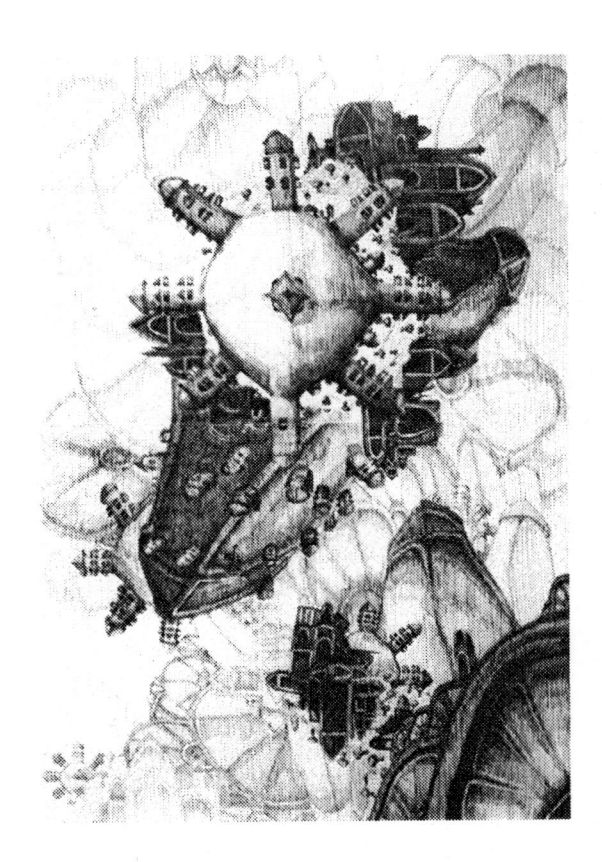

VALUES/VALUE JUDGMENTS

Man's judgments of value follow directly his wishes for happiness—they are an attempt to support his illusions with arguments.
Sigmund Freud

The ultimate disease of our times is valuelessness.
Abraham Maslow

VENGEFULNESS

The great secret, the deeply buried mystery of the apparent apathy to crime and to proposals for better controlling crime, lies in the persistent, intrusive wish for vengeance.
Karl Menninger

VIOLENCE/FORCE

A person displaying violence on film is as influential as one displaying it in real life.
Albert Bandura

Our one tool of diplomacy appears to be force or the threat of force. We seem to have forgotten that there is such a thing as negotiation and communication.
Carl Rogers

More violence on the part of society will make more violence on the part of those it can't control.
Karl Menninger

With the advent of ever more deadly forms of weaponry, as the price of survival humans must free themselves from reliance on violence as the ultimate means of power.
Jerome Frank

Destructiveness is the outcome of unlived lives.
Erich Fromm

If we can stop destroying ourselves we may stop destroying others. We have to begin by admitting and even accepting our violence, rather than blindly destroying ourselves with it, and therewith we have to realize that we are as deeply afraid to live and to love as we are to die.
R. D. Laing

The extremes of 'brutal' behavior are confined to man and there is no parallel in nature to our savage treatment of each other. We are the cruelest and most ruthless species that has ever walked the earth.
Anthony Storr

So we seldom look for the common denominator, what we have in common, but we look for where we are different, so that we can hate and kill each other.
Fritz Perls

In urban, industrial societies, there are far too many people who feel humiliated, ineffective, inadequate, and of no account. It is from their ranks that the majority of those who commit acts of violence are drawn; and it is toward giving such people a sense of value and significance that more of our best efforts ought to be directed.
Anthony Storr

W-X-Y-Z

WAR/PEACE

As soon as it is possible for a small group of fanatics to manufacture nuclear weapons in their own bathtub, I am reasonably sure several of them will get together and deliberately use these weapons against the rest of us, in the name of God, Jesus, Mohammed, or what you will.
Albert Ellis

We can communicate anywhere in the world instantly by satellite. We can fly across the Atlantic in three hours—a trip that took several weeks, 100 years ago. We have also created the biggest monster of all time—the nuclear bomb. We still haven't learned to accept a positive way of dealing with conflict.
Virginia Satir

War today would mean the sheer extermination of one of the combatants, if not both. This is so true, so obvious, that we can but wonder why the conduct of war is not banned by general consent.
Sigmund Freud

What possible difference can a new approach to family life or to psychotherapy make when our very planet is threatened with dissolution?. We cannot face the fact that our world—the planet earth—is in mortal danger.
Carl Rogers

Men have brought their powers of subduing the forces of nature to such a pitch that by using them, they could now very easily exterminate one another to the last man. They know this—hence arises a great part of their current unrest, their dejection, their mood of apprehension.
Sigmund Freud

These two factors—man's cultural disposition and well-founded fear of the form that future wars will take—may serve to put an end to war…but by what ways or byways this will come about, we cannot guess.
Sigmund Freud (in a letter to Albert Einstein)

Every move we make in fear of the next war in fact hastens it.
Gregory Bateson

The abolition of war will be extremely difficult but there is no choice.
Jerome Frank

Peacemaking,…requires a call to action.
M. Scott Peck

As the world's people demand freedom and self-determination it is urgent that we learn how diverse communities of empowered individuals, with the freedom to construct their own stories and identities, might live together in mutual peace.
Maureen O'Hara

WEEPING/CRYING

Weeping is perhaps the most human and universal of all relief measures.
Karl Menninger

WILL

We love and will the world as an immediate, spontaneous totality. We will the world, create it by our decision, our fiat, our choice; and we love it, give it affect, energy, power to love and change us as we mold and change it. This is what it means to be fully related to one's world.
Rollo May

I believe the will is the Cinderella of modern psychology. It has been relegated to the kitchen.
Roberto Assagioli

If you have only "will" and no "wish," you have the dried-up, Victorian, neo-puritan man. If you have only "wish" and no "will," you have the driven, unfree, infantile person who, as an adult,...may become the robot man.
Rollo May

I can will knowledge, but not wisdom; going to bed, but not sleeping; eating, but not hunger; meekness, but not humility; scrupulosity, but not virtue; self-assertion or bravado, but not courage; lust, but not love; commiseration, but not sympathy; congratulations, but not admiration; religiosity, but not faith; reading, but not understanding.
Leslie Farber

CARL WHITAKER (1912–1995)

Carl Whitaker is the founder of the experiential/symbolic approach to family therapy. His career in the field of psychotherapy began quite indirectly. Because of personnel shortages Whitaker, a trained obstetrician/gynecologist, received a postgraduate fellowship and was credited toward board eligibility in psychiatry. His first placement was as a resident psychiatric administrator in a small diagnostic hospital. He later learned play therapy in a child guidance clinic, before being appointed to the psychiatry faculty at the University of Louisville. His job was to teach medical students to do psychotherapy. Since he knew virtually nothing about psychotherapy nor about psychiatric patients he adapted his knowledge of child therapy to his work with adolescents and adults. From 1944 to 1946 he worked as a psychiatrist for the understaffed Oak Ridge Hospital, the site of the Manhattan Project during World War II. His inexperience and stress led him to the idea of using co therapists. Subsequently he established and became chairperson of the department of psychiatry in the medical school at Emory University where he gained national recognition for his use of treating schizophrenics with an aggressive kind of play therapy. Whitaker worked in private practice for a time, and eventually took a position at the University of Wisconsin Medical School as a professor of psychiatry where he focused on family therapy.

He has developed a therapy in which he teases people to be in contact with their absurdity. He is a Don Quixote who challenges you to see that you are charging your own windmills…I do it differently, but essentially, like him, I am a challenger of people's reality.
Salvatore Minuchin

Most important for Whitaker was his enjoyment in what he was doing while being extremely effective with patients. If therapists can find this part of themselves, they may feel about therapy the way Mickey Mantle did about baseball when he said, "And they pay me for this too!"
Len Bergantino

WOMEN

The roots of most women's problems are political and social. The solution to such political problems must be revolutionary rather than psychotherapeutic.
Sheldon Kopp

As much as women want to be good scientists or engineers, they want first and foremost to be womanly companions of men and to be mothers.
Bruno Bettelheim

My experience confirms that the vast majority of women have been sexually abused in childhood. In both my psychotherapy practice and among my friends, recollection of the trauma frequently occurs later in

life, often in an attempt to explain seemingly irrational fears that have plagued the individual for a lifetime.
Peter R. Breggin

In taking up a masculine calling, studying, and working in a man's way, woman is doing something not wholly in agreement with if not directly injurious to her feminine nature.
C. G. Jung

Your young girls...are not happy with their American husbands because they are not afraid of them. It is natural, even though it is archaic, for women to want to be afraid when they love.
C. G. Jung (1912)

Work and love—these are the basics. Without them there is neurosis.
Theodore Reik

A considerable number of persons are able to protect themselves against the outbreak of serious neurotic phenomena only through intense work.
Karl Abraham

WORLD

The world gets much prettier as it gets more complicated.
Gregory Bateson

About the Author

THE EDITOR:
Bernard Nisenholz Ed.D., is Professor Emeritus at California State University Northridge. He currently resides in Westlake Village, CA.

THE ARTIST:
Lyle Nisenholz is an artist and teacher currently residing in Tokyo, Japan. He received his B.A. in art from University of California Santa Barbara.

Index

A

Abraham, Karl (Psychoanalyst), 4, 5, 8, 10, 24, 39, 40, 43, 54, 55, 56, 57, 61, 73, 78, 79, 85, 90, 91, 105, 118, 128, 131, 135, 136, 137, 149, 156
Adler, Alfred (Founder of Individual Therapy), 10, 11, 15, 16, 17, 39, 46, 57, 63, 69, 74, 77, 78, 82, 85, 87, 91, 93, 98, 99, 105, 112, 122, 123, 127, 141, 146
Allen, Woody (Comedian), 6, 38, 81, 94, 99, 118
Allport, Gordon (Psychologist), 49
Anderson, Carol, 112
Anonymous, 94, 106
Arbuckle, Dugald S. (psychologist), 108
Assagioli, Roberto (Founder of Psychosynthesis), 18, 38, 48, 54, 84, 141, 154
Auden, W. H. (Poet), 9, 118
Axelrad, Albert S. (Rabbi), 86

B

Bateson, Gregory (Anthropologist and Family Therapist), 93, 94, 153, 157
Beck, Aaron (Founder of Cognitive Behavior Therapy), 113, 133
Behrman, S. N. (Author), 118
Bergantino, Len (Psychologist), 119, 155
Berne, Eric (Founder of Transactional Analysis), 3, 18, 21, 25, 26, 27, 30, 31, 32, 33, 38, 46, 47, 51, 76, 82, 106, 107, 108, 112, 113, 138
Bettelheim, Bruno (Psychoanalyst), 28, 35, 130, 147, 155

Binswanger, Ludwig (Psychoanalyst), 32, 124
Blanton, Smiley (Psychiatrist), 83
Bloch, Erbst (Gernan Marxist philosopher and atheist theologian), 67
Bloom, Harold (Author and literary critic), 4
Boss, Mildred (MD), 49
Breggin, Peter (Psychiatrist), 6, 100, 106, 113, 118, 156
Breuer, Joseph (Physician), 2
Brossard, Chandler (Author), 44
Bruehl, Elisabeth Young (Psychoanalyst), 14
Bube, Martin (Philosopher), 5, 37, 42, 55, 58, 81, 83, 89, 93, 104, 105, 116, 127, 130, 146, 148
Bugental, James (Ph.D. Existential Humanistic Therapist), 33, 58, 80, 87, 100, 128, 134, 144
Burns, David (Psychiatrist), 130

C

Caplan, Paula, 5
Capra, Fritjof (Physicist and Systems Theorist), 67, 76, 125
Carkhuff, Robert (Psychologist), 54
Chesler, Phyllis (Psychologist), 5, 117
Coles, Robert (Developmental Psychologist), 44
Conger, John P., 70, 123

D

Dass, Ram (Philosopher), 103
Dreikers, Rudolph, 141

Dreikurs, Rudolph (Adlerian Psychologist), 91, 127, 128

E

Eagle, Dana (Comedian), 93
Egan, Gerald (Priest and Psychotherapist), 116
Ellis, Albert (Founder of Rational Emotive Behavior Therapy), 17, 52, 81, 82, 126, 129, 130, 134, 152
English, Fanita (MSW), 15, 27, 75, 87
Enright, John B., 116
Erickson, Milton (MD Pioneer of medical hypnosis), 34, 74, 112, 121
Erikson, Erik, 17, 26, 30, 40, 44, 57, 107, 138
Evans, Richard (Social Psychologist), 70, 144
Eysenck, Hans (Behavioral Psychologist), 7

F

Farber, Leslie H. (Psychiatrist), 61, 154
Farson, Richard (Psychologist), 133
Feenberg, Andrew (Philosopher), 126
Fenichel, Otto (Psychoanalyst), 39, 114
Ferenczi, Sandor (Psychoanalyst), 100, 111, 116, 117
Frank, Jerome (Psychiatrist), 38, 81, 107, 109, 120, 136, 144, 150, 153
Frankl, Viktor (Founder of Logotherapy), 29, 32, 34, 46, 48, 49, 56, 58, 63, 79, 80, 81, 88, 121, 143, 146
Franz, Marie-Louise von (Psychologist), 68
Freud, Jacob, 1
Freud, Sigmund (Psychoanalyst), 1, 2, 3, 4, 5, 6, 7, 8, 9, 10, 11, 12, 13, 14, 15, 16, 17, 18, 19, 20, 21, 23, 24, 27, 28, 29, 32, 33, 34, 36, 37, 39, 40, 41, 44, 47, 49, 50, 51, 52, 56, 58, 59, 63, 65, 66, 67, 69, 77, 80, 81, 82, 83, 85, 88, 89, 90, 92, 94, 95, 100, 110, 118, 119, 122, 123, 125, 126, 129, 130, 134, 137, 144, 149, 153
Friedman, Maurice (Professor Emeritus of religious studies, philosophy and comparative literature), 5, 68
Fromm, Erich (Psychoanalyst), 7, 13, 25, 26, 36, 52, 54, 56, 57, 67, 70, 78, 80, 81, 82, 83, 84, 85, 89, 92, 98, 105, 114, 115, 126, 150

G

Gaylin, William (Psychiatrist), 9, 61, 89
Gendlin, Eugene (Psychologist and Philosopher), 60, 105, 134
Gilligan, Carol (Psychologist), 13
Ginott, Hiam (Child Psychologist), 30, 63, 97
Glasser, William (Founder of Reality Therapy), 26, 51, 57, 110, 116, 131, 143
Goldblatt, David, 112
Goleman, Daniel (Writer), 7
Goodyear, Rodney K. (Psychologist), 134
Goulding, Mary (MSW, Psychotherapist), 108
Greben, Stanley (Psychiatrist), 113, 117
Green, Arnold W. (Sociologist), 133
Greening, Tom (Psychologist), 8, 140
Greenspan, Miriam (Mental Health Counselor), 13, 121
Greer, Germaine (Author), 5
Grof, Stanislav (Transpersonal Psychologist), 92
Grosskurth, Phyllis (Psychologist), 6, 11
Guerin, Phil (Family Therapist), 95
Guntrip, Harry (Psychoanalyst), 21, 120

H

Haley, Jay (Family Therapist), 90, 118
Hall, Calvin (Psychologist), 4

Heilbrun, Carolyn (Author), 50
Hesse, Hermann (Author), 67
Hillman, James James (Jungian Analyst), 16, 107, 109, 128, 138, 141
Hoffman, Edward (Psychologist), 103
Horney, Karen (Psychoanalyst), 3, 55, 58, 78, 85, 92, 106, 120

J

Jaffé, Aniela, 68
James, William (Psychologist and Philosopher), 8, 16, 33, 58, 80, 87, 100, 113, 122, 126, 128, 144
Janov, Arthur (Founder of Primal Therapy), 91, 108
Jaspers, Karl (Psychologist and philosopher), 58, 105
Jones, Ernest (Psychoanalyst), 3, 6, 29, 34, 123
Jourard, Sidney (Psychologist), 57, 88, 115, 127
Jung, C. G. (Founder of Analytical Psychology), 9, 10, 11, 15, 16, 18, 21, 29, 30, 34, 35, 36, 38, 40, 45, 48, 52, 53, 54, 57, 58, 61, 62, 63, 65, 66, 67, 68, 69, 70, 71, 72, 73, 74, 77, 79, 80, 83, 85, 88, 90, 91, 95, 96, 97, 105, 106, 110, 112, 117, 120, 123, 136, 137, 142, 146, 148, 156

K

Kaiser, Helmuth, 99
Karier, Clarence, 70
Keen, Sam (Philosopher and author), 4
Kempler, Walter (Family Therapist), 107, 120
Kirchenbaum, Howard, 134
Klein, Melanie (Psychoanalyst), 39, 49, 50, 119
Kohut, Heinz (Founder of Self-Psychology), 74, 115

Kopp, Sheldon (Psychotherapist), 52, 53, 76, 78, 83, 92, 99, 106, 111, 123, 127, 128, 146, 155
Kraus, Karl (Viennesse dramatist, critic and satirist), 41, 118
Kreyche, Gerald (Philosopher), 49

L

Laing, R. D. (Psychiatrist), 3, 8, 31, 34, 43, 47, 52, 71, 73, 74, 75, 84, 89, 92, 93, 106, 111, 116, 124, 135, 146, 148, 150
Langs, Robert (Psychoanalyst), 121
Lazarus, Arnold (Founder of Multimodal Therapy), 73, 120
Levant, Oscar (Pianist), 5
Lindner, Robert (Psychoanalyst), 34
Lowe, Marshall. C., 133
Lowen, Alexander (MD, Founder of Bioenergetics), 28, 29, 40, 46, 89, 93, 96, 115, 124, 125, 127, 129

M

Mahler, Margaret (Psychoanalyst), 36
Malcolm, Janet (Writer and Journalist), 96, 134
Mann, Thomas (Author), 4
Maslow, Abraham (Psychologist), 4, 5, 8, 24, 39, 40, 43, 54, 55, 56, 57, 61, 73, 78, 79, 85, 86, 90, 105, 118, 128, 131, 135, 136, 137, 149
Masson, Jeffrey Moussaieff (Psychoanalyst), 8, 45, 71, 104, 108, 109, 110, 113, 116, 121, 133, 140
May, Rollo (Psychologist), 16, 17, 28, 29, 32, 33, 36, 38, 39, 52, 58, 59, 64, 79, 80, 81, 82, 85, 87, 94, 97, 110, 112, 114, 127, 136, 142, 146, 154
Menninger, Karl (Psychiatrist), 37, 56, 88, 91, 93, 143, 149, 150, 154
Miller, Alice (Pychiatriat), 5, 117

Minuchin, Salvatore (Family Therapist), 46, 95, 96, 97, 119, 121, 135, 155
Mitchell, Julian, 5
Moreno, Zerka (Co-founder of Psychodrama), 41, 88
Morita, Shoma (Founder of Morita Therapy), 47
Mosak, Harold H. (Adlerian Psychologist), 16
Moustakas, Clark (Psychologist), 22, 55, 79, 81, 124, 136, 148
Murray, Henry A. (Psychoanalyst), 104, 120

N

Nabokov, Vladimir (Author), 6, 99
Napier, Augustus (Family therapist), 6, 119
Nin, Anais (Author), 122

P

Palazzoli, Mara Selvini (Family Therapist), 111
Papp, Peggy (Family Therapist), 96, 114
Parlour, Richard. R., 145
Peck, M. Scott (Psychiatrist), 29, 43, 55, 61, 64, 99, 110, 153
Perls, Fritz (Founder of Gestalt Therapy), 4, 6, 8, 17, 24, 28, 29, 36, 39, 41, 45, 48, 55, 56, 84, 86, 87, 91, 97, 100, 101, 102, 103, 104, 114, 121, 124, 125, 127, 131, 135, 136, 137, 141, 150
Perls, Laura (Co-founder of Gestalt Therapy), 28, 30, 33, 62, 80, 103
Polster, Erving (Psychologist), 122

R

Rank, Otto (Psychoanalyst), 24, 53, 56, 70, 79, 89, 90, 91, 100, 122, 123, 142
Reich, Wilhelm (Psychoanalyst), 8, 24, 46, 47, 49, 72, 89, 101, 118, 124, 125, 126, 137

Reik, Theodore (Psychoanalyst), 3, 32, 80, 82, 83, 94, 108, 112, 117, 127, 156
Resnick, Robert W., 111
Rogers, Carl (Founder of Person Centered Therapy), 4, 8, 35, 43, 58, 74, 76, 77, 81, 83, 85, 88, 91, 100, 106, 107, 108, 111, 119, 120, 122, 123, 124, 132, 133, 134, 140, 142, 150, 153
Roustang, Francois (Psychoanalyst), 11
Rubin, William, 99
Rudmin, Floyd Webster (Ph.D. Psychologist), 16

S

Sabbagh, Karl, 145
Sagan, Carl (Astronomer), 3
Satir, Virginia (Family Therapist), 4, 39, 46, 58, 78, 110, 114, 126, 135, 152
Schneider, Kirk, 75
Schur, Edwin (Sociologist), 27, 137, 145
Schutz, William, 45, 102, 111, 125, 130, 146
Searles, Harold, 38, 93
Semrad, Elvin (Psychiatrist), 28
Shapiro, Arthur K., 107, 119
Shepard, Martin, 102
Shoales, Ian (Author and commentator), 6
Shostrom, Everett (Founder of Actualizing Therapy), 45, 82, 133, 140
Shur, Edwin, 51
Simon, Richard, 95
Skinner, B. F. (Behavioral Psychologist), 8, 18, 32, 35, 36, 43, 45, 47, 59, 76, 77, 95, 104, 119, 132, 138, 139, 140, 141, 142
Sontag, Susan (Author), 89
Stein, Paul, 71
Steiner, Claude (Clinical Psychologist), 21, 27
Stekhel, Wilhelm (Psychoanalyst), 94
Storr, Anthony (Psychiatrist), 143, 150, 151
Strupp, Hans (Psychoanalyst), 107

Sullivan, Hary S. (Psychiatrist), 62, 97, 114, 144
Szasz, Thomas (Psychiatrist and psychotherapy critic), 9, 11, 13, 30, 37, 48, 52, 56, 67, 86, 90, 99, 104, 110, 117, 129, 130, 145

T

Taft, Jessie, 122
Tarachow, Sidney (Psychoanalyst), 17
Travis, Carol (Psychiatrist), 75
Trilling, Lionel (Writer), 4, 9

V

Viscott, David (Radio Psychologist), 18, 26, 76

W

Watson, John B. (Behavioral Psychologist), 9
Watzlawick, Paul (Family Therapist), 123
Wehr, Gerhard (Jung biographer), 67, 70
Weinberg, George, 109
Wells, H. G. (Author), 67

Wescott, Joan, 76
Wheelis, Allen (Psychoanalyst), 38, 81, 94, 99
Whitaker, Carl (Family Therapist), 46, 116, 120, 154, 155
Whitmont, Edward C. (M.D. Psychotherapist and Homeopath), 67
Wilden, Anthony, 109
Williams, Tennessee (Author), 111
Wilson, Colin (Author), 49
Winnicott, D. W., 94, 96, 97
Wolf-Man, The, 7
Wren, Gilbert C., 113

Y

Yalom, Irvin (Psychiatrist), 9, 39, 62, 78, 79, 86, 103, 114, 115, 116, 127

Z

Zilbergeld, Bernie (M. D. Psychologist), 6, 74, 104, 109, 110, 144

978-0-595-39659-7
0-595-39659-3

Printed in the United Kingdom
by Lightning Source UK Ltd.
115760UKS00001B/319